LACEMAKING

MAT FOR TRAY

Worked by Mrs. Dixon, Clapham, Beds. Design by C. C. Channer

LACEMAKING
Point Ground

C. C. CHANNER
revised by
M. WALLER

DRYAD PRESS LTD
LONDON

First published 1928

ISBN 08521 9612 1

Printed in Great Britain by
Butler & Tanner Ltd
Frome, Somerset
for the publishers
Dryad Press Ltd
4 Fitzhardinge Street
London W1H 0AH

CONTENTS

Preface to the Revised Edition

Miss C. C. Channer held a high position in the world of lacemaking, and although I never had the pleasure of meeting her I feel that I have known her by talking with her friends and pupils. Much of my knowledge of Point Ground lace has been gained from her book, "Practical Lacemaking". It was, as its name implied, a practical book, and with the renewed interest in the craft the new edition should be welcome. In its preparation I have been guided firstly by present-day conditions, and secondly by experience gained in teaching others. It has been necessary to make certain alterations to allow for the difference in equipment available in 1928, *the time of the first edition, and that available today.*

The wording in the instructional chapters has been condensed to main essentials and the chapter On Teaching Lacemaking omitted. Two lessons: Honeycomb filling and French Ground insertion, have been replaced by Honeycomb edging and a French Ground edging, as they teach the same principle but have a more practical use. Separate patterns have not been included in a folder as in the first edition. Planning on sectional paper preserves them in a more permanent form and each pattern can be copied as required with a greater degree of accuracy. Otherwise I have endeavoured to keep the book as near to the original form as possible.

It will be noted that the word "Bucks" has now been deleted from the title. The original title may have given the impression that this type of lace is exclusive to the county of Buckinghamshire, whereas it belongs equally to Bedfordshire and Northamptonshire. Other countries: e.g. Spain and Denmark, have also published practical lacemaking books including patterns for this type of lace. Although each county or country may have its own distinctive patterns, the principles involved in the making of the lace are the same throughout. Apart from the title, I have also been able to clarify one or two practical details, which I hope will eliminate any misunderstanding in the working of the lace.

I offer my thanks to those who have helped to check the instructions in the revised version and to those of Miss Channer's friends who have given me much helpful advice. Without their help I could not with confidence have submitted the book for re-publication as a practical book on Lacemaking.

M. Waller

Introduction

PLACE names for lace make a tantalizing problem. At some particular period the lace made in a certain district becomes famous and the name of that district is attached to that kind of lace. The lace is copied in a dozen other districts and other names come to be applied to the same type of lace. Again, a different kind of lace begins to be made in the district and in time the district name is applied to a different lace. Here is material for endless puzzles. To the lacemaker the only satisfactory name is one that suggests the nature of the work, but of such names there are very few. In the 18th and 19th centuries the counties of Buckinghamshire, Bedfordshire and Northamptonshire became well known for making a certain kind of lace locally called "point ground" or "half-stitch lace". This lace is known abroad as "Point de Lille"; it spread into Huntingdonshire and to Oxfordshire; it was also made in Wiltshire, in Yorkshire, in Sussex, possibly in other places now forgotten. Its characteristic is a net ground formed of twisted threads connected by what lacemakers call a "half-stitch". The pattern is defined by a thick thread called a gimp, though the more solid types of pattern can be worked without a gimp. The ground and the pattern are worked at the same time, not separately as in Honiton lace.

Buckinghamshire and Bedfordshire lace is also associated with another kind of lace which was introduced from the Mediterranean region during the 19th century. It is locally known as "Maltese". This little book is intended as a guide to the making of the "point ground" lace, and includes the "French ground", "wire ground" or "kat stitch", known on the Continent as "Point de Paris". This latter is similar to "point ground" in every particular, except that the ground is worked with "whole stitches" on a slightly different system.

Probably lace was made in the Southern Midland counties long before the introduction of "point ground". In the 16th and 17th centuries it was evidently a widespread craft, though certain districts and certain countries became more distinguished than others for lace. Northamptonshire has a lace known as Katherine of Aragon lace; it is unlike any other local lace and has a Flemish-Spanish character. There is a tradition that Queen Katherine taught lace to the villagers when she lived in Bedfordshire. Other traditions suggest that lacemaking took deep root in the Southern Midlands owing to settlements of Flemish refugees. There is nothing surprising in the fact that special handicrafts passed from one European country to another, just as modern manufactures do.

It seems probable that most of the designs used were brought from Flanders. English designers altered and adapted designs but did not originate many. I once questioned some old lace designers in Bucks and Northants about pricking the "ground". I was told they took the ground from the "cards". I said "Where did you get the cards?" and the answer was "Oh, we always had them". I imagine that they were brought from Flanders. The cards in question were pieces of white card pricked all over with holes as required for working the net ground. They were in different sized meshes. In arranging a pattern the designers used the cards to prick the ground the size they required. As I could not discover how the cards were made, I and some others puzzled it out for ourselves, and in this book I venture to tell lacemakers how to prick the ground from sectional paper if they do not possess "the cards". It is interesting work and it makes one wonder at the technical perfection and ingenuity of the old designers. They are indeed hard to beat, and it is an education in lacemaking and designing to study and work out old parchments.

VARIETIES OF LACE

LACE is a big subject, much bigger than many people imagine. This book tries to open the doors to one only of the many, many forms of lace. Point ground is not the easiest kind to learn, but it teaches much and lays a good foundation for others.

How can we define lace? The word brings before one's mind something intricate with a pattern in it; something with holes like net work; an ornamental edging like a fringe, which suggests some of the various types of lace. Great ingenuity has been shown in the effort to produce the airy fabric known as lace, and many different methods have been used in order to produce the effects sought by lacemakers. First there is net, a thread knotted to make a fishing net, something strong yet open. A net ornamented by needle and thread gives us "filet lace". Then there is the word "lace" in its older meaning, a lace such as a shoe lace, threads plaited together to make a cord. These threads plaited in an ornamental and elaborate way give us lace edgings and insertions. Then a fringe; the threads from a piece of woven stuff may be knotted into an ornamental fringe; the same effect may be obtained by plaiting and knotting threads on a pillow and then sewing it to the material. Now let us go further and introduce another word, embroidery; at once we call to mind many other types of lace. We work with needle and thread on a piece of woven linen, cutting away the foundation till little is left but the embroidery; the result is lace. Then we make our embroidery stitches with the needle and thread without the linen foundation, and there is needlepoint lace. Such lace is often hard to distinguish from pillow lace of plaited threads. One lace constantly imitates another. The introduction of machinery suggests in the modern world still further types imitating the older laces, and yet still thought of as handwork. Pillow laces in the course of centuries developed a net work of their own, very different from the earlier knotted net. Pillow net is formed by twisting and plaiting large numbers of threads. These, imitated by machine work, give a net which could be embroidered, hence tambour work and net darning.

Yet this is not the end. The solid parts of the older laces could be made separately in small pieces, and then sewn on to the machine made net, hence the various types of appliqué laces, such as Honiton and Brussels. Still there is another method. Instead of the solid pattern being made on the pillow, a piece of muslin is laid over the net and the parts not needed to form the pattern are cut away, the edges of the pattern being first firmly sewn to the net, as in Carrickmacross and Swiss lace.

We have not mentioned all; there is tape lace too, a form of needlepoint into which a tape or braid is introduced to lessen the work. It belongs to the class of laces in which there is a machine-made element, as in appliqué and embroidered net.

Laces that are entirely handwork may be divided into two great classes, needlepoint, and pillow lace, though the two are sometimes combined.

Pillow laces, again, fall into two big divisions, those in which the ground and pattern are woven in in one piece, and those in which the pattern is worked in separate parts and joined afterwards, or connected at intervals during the process of working. Point ground lace has a net ground woven in one with the pattern which is often outlined by a thick thread woven in at the same time.

Would-be students of pillow lacemaking often ask which lace should be learnt first. The answer depends on the purpose in view and on the personal taste of the student. Torchon and Cluny or simple Italian and Bruge will supply an effective coarse lace which will not be difficult or slow. Honiton or Fine Brussels will require great concentration and considerable time spent on it.

Another question asked is, Can one learn from a book? It is possible, but the best of books cannot foresee all the difficulties so that one or two personal lessons are a tremendous help and will make the book more intelligible.

APPARATUS FOR LACEMAKING

Pillows

Two kinds of pillows were in general use in the South Midlands lace district, a "square" pillow, which, with the corners rounded off, sometimes resembled a ball, and the

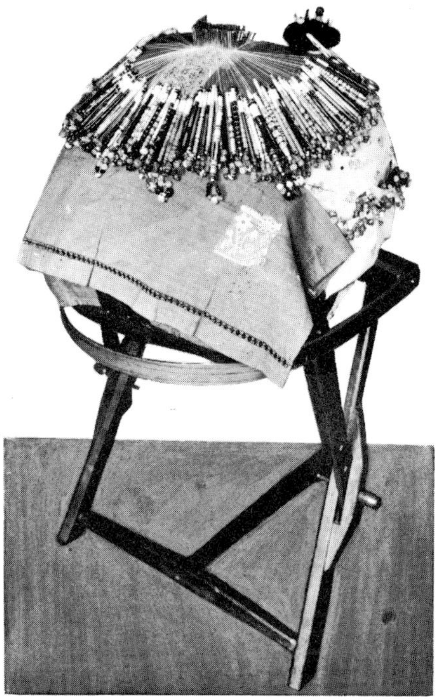

Buckinghamshire lace pillow with pattern set in.

"round" pillow which resembled a bolster. Both were made of straw arranged in wisps and hammered hard with a mallet. They are both still used today but as they are very heavy, stands, known as "lace horses" or "maids" are used. The maids are of two kinds, those which help to support the pillow while it rests on the worker's lap, and those which have a "bow", a kind of bracket which takes the whole weight of the pillow, and on which it can be left standing. A "maid" of the first kind can very well be replaced by using the back of a chair, the seat being turned away from the worker.

In different countries pillows have developed in different ways. In Belgium the straw pillow has been given a wooden foundation and fixed to an adjustable stand. Another type with a wooden foundation has been evolved to stand on a table sloping like a desk. In the French pillow, the pillow has been

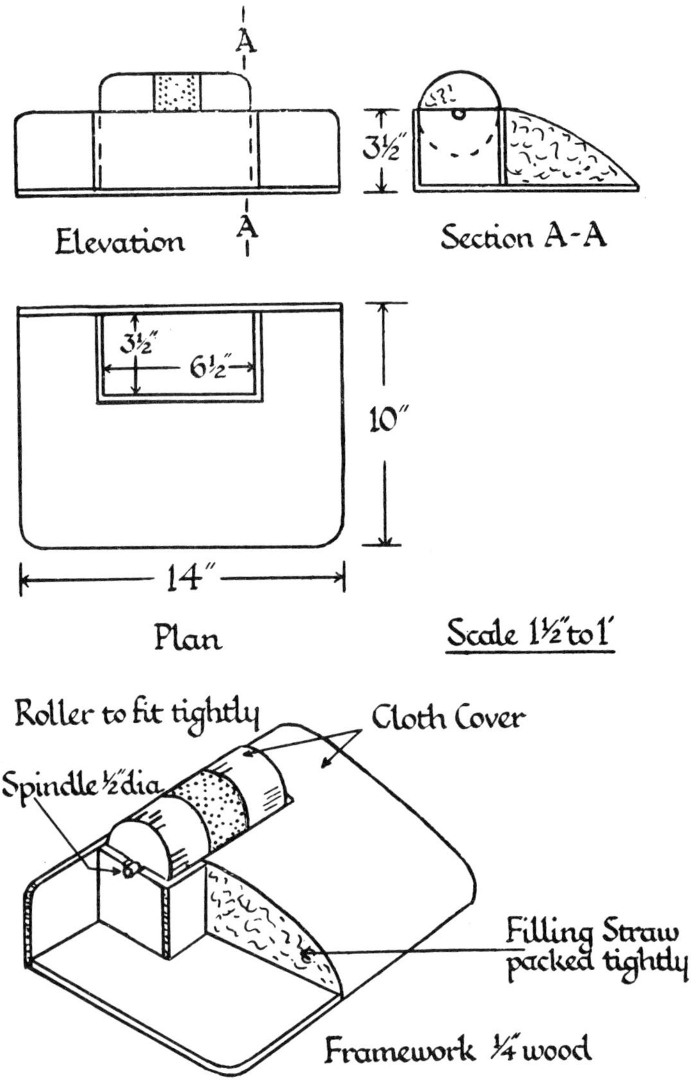

How to make a pillow of the French type.

reduced to a roller fixed into a wooden framework and surrounded with a sloping cushion on which the bobbins rest. This type is only suitable for edgings.

At the present time it is difficult to obtain pillows of any description. The diagrams on page 14 show how to make a pillow of the French type. A cushion type may be made as follows: Prepare a square bag of unbleached calico or hessian (18″ square is a convenient size) and fill with wood wool or packing straw. The important thing in making either type is to hammer the stuffing and to pack in sufficient so that the pillow is extremely hard. If it is at all soft the pins will not hold firm when working. Dried sawdust can be used as a filling but it is apt to "bed" down after a time and soften the surface of the pillow.

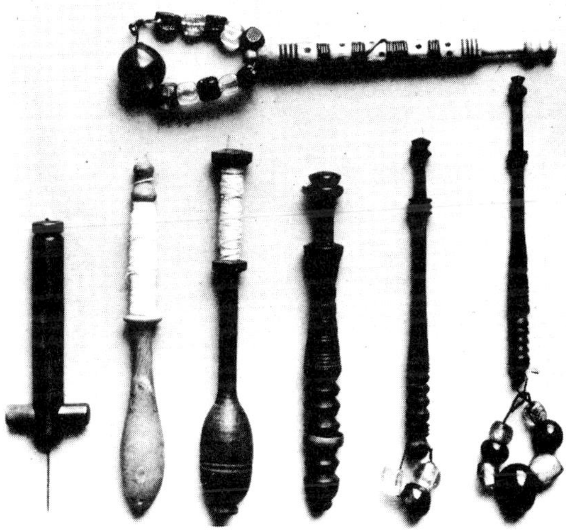

Varieties of bobbins and a pricker.

Bobbins

Bobbins used in the Midlands are mostly of wood or bone, having a head to hold the hitched thread, and a ring of beads to weight the shaft. During the 19th century an amazing amount of skill and ingenuity was used in ornamenting them. They were turned in a variety of patterns, some inlaid with various woods, some had brass wire round them, some were studded with pewter, while others were coloured and covered with names and inscriptions. Bobbins belonging to an earlier period are of a simpler design, having flat heads and thick stumpy bodies with no beads to steady them. A type of bobbin used in Belgium also has a flat head not used for hitching the thread and the handle bulges to a sort of knob at the end, which answers the same purpose as the English beads. The French bobbin has a head like the modern English bobbin, and a short bulging handle.

Pins

Lace pins are made of brass; other kinds will rust in the pillow and cause ironmould on the lace. The yellow variety should be used to avoid confusion. A convenient size is $1\frac{1}{8}''$ but for finer laces use either $1\frac{3}{8}''$ or $\frac{7}{8}''$. The shorter pins do not bend so easily and will be found easier to handle by the beginner. The old lacemakers ornamented their head and foot pins with coloured sealing wax and beads.

Patterns or Parchments

The name, parchment, is derived from the fact that the older patterns were pricked on a parchment or vellum skin. Nowadays a special glazed card is used. In order to prick the pattern the following equipment is also required:

1. Sectional paper to mark out the pattern; 1/10, 1/12, and 1/16 are the most useful sizes.
2. A pricker, which can be made by inserting a darning needle into a handle of wood.
3. A pad of felt or blanket on which to prick.

Equipment for dressing the pillow

On English pillows, either square or round, the parchment is pinned on to the middle of the pillow; a working cloth is laid over the part where the bobbins will lie and is lowered as the work proceeds. The upper part is also covered with a cloth so that the worked lace and parchment may be kept clean. When the lower end of the parchment is reached, the bobbins must be pinned firmly into the cloth, which is turned up over them. All pins are removed, care being taken that the weight of the bobbins is not on the lace. The lace and bobbins are moved up and pinned out on the pattern at the top of the parchment. The process is called "*setting up*". Beginning a pattern is called "*setting in*".

The French pillows do not require working cloths. The pattern is fitted round the roller so that the design is continuous. If the parchment fits too loosely, it can be padded to fit correctly by wrapping soft woollen material round the roller.

Thread

For point ground lace a fine cotton thread was used. The most usual size was known as 10 slip. The skein was divided up by red cotton into the number denoting the size, e.g. 6 slip was divided into 6 groups, 10 slip into 10 and so on. A 200 linen thread would be equivalent to a 10 slip cotton but unfortunately neither is being manufactured at the present time. D.M.C. thread No. 80, although highly mercerised, seems to be a good substitute. Gimp thread, which is a soft shiny linen thread, is used to outline the pattern.

The following scale suggests threads which can be used for each size graph on which the pattern is marked.

Graph	Knox linen thread 2 cord	D.M.C.	Gimp
1/10	100	30	12
1/12	150	60	18
1/16	200	80	24

This is only intended to serve as a rough estimate; when the worker has gained experience she will be able to experiment for herself on other size graph with any size thread she may have. As a general rule it is not advisable to work point ground patterns in anything coarser than 100 linen thread. A bobbin winder is useful but not essential as the bobbins can be wound by hand.

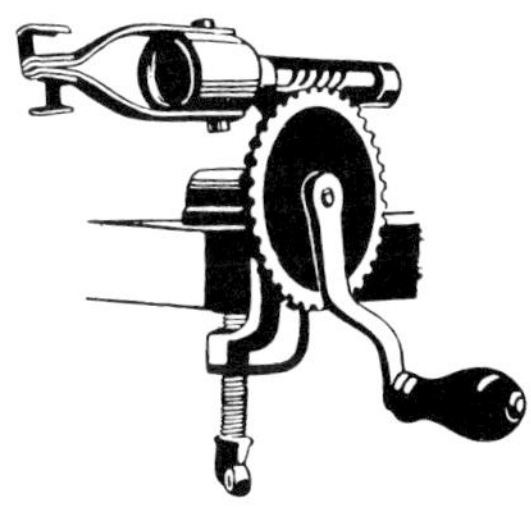

ON PRICKING PARCHMENTS

WITH the exception of one or two, each pattern is worked out on a sectional chart so that the worker can copy and prick her own pattern. By following a few simple rules it should be possible to do this without a knowledge of the principles underlying the method of designing for point ground lace.

1. Choose the thread and appropriate graph paper as given in the chapter on Equipment. For the complete novice it might be advisable to start the first pattern with 1/10 graph and 100 linen thread.

2. Using a fine-pointed H or HB pencil, dot out the pattern on to a length of graph paper. This should be done very accurately. Take particular notice where each dot should be; whether on the intersection of the lines or, if on a line between the intersection, whether it is half way or a quarter. The finished lace depends upon using a good pricking and accuracy in doing this cannot be stressed too often.

3. Attach the paper firmly to a piece of pricking card. This may be done by sticking the paper with paste at intervals of 2 or 3 inches or by binding the edges with small pieces of sellotape at similar intervals. The paper should be sufficiently firm to prevent it slipping even the smallest fraction while pricking.

4. Lay the card over a pad of felt or blanket and prick through each dot. The best results will be obtained by holding the pricker vertically and by allowing only the point of the pricker to enter the card. If the holes are too large the pins will not hold firmly when working and the finished lace will be inferior. Remove the paper and copy any gimp lines on to the card with ink.

In the old days of village lace schools, the pricking of parchments from drafts was done on flat sheets of lead with a strong fine awl. When the lead became much marked with the awl it could be melted and run smooth again. The sheets were spoken of as "leads". When they ceased to be used they were sold and melted down for other purposes, so few, if any have survived.

When copying the more advanced patterns it will be helpful to know something of the method used in designing point ground patterns. The basis of the point ground is the distinctive net or Point de Lille as it is known abroad. One variation of the net is Point de Paris, French Wire ground or Kat stitch and another variation used as a filling with the point ground is Honeycomb ground known abroad as Point de Mariage. Whichever ground is used, the pattern is woven into the net so that before making any design for this type of lace it is necessary to learn to prick the net. This is done as follows:

Take a sheet of sectional paper and with a sharp H or HB pencil make dots down any line at intersections of the lines. Make other rows of dots $1\frac{1}{2}$ squares away to the left. The second row of dots will be halfway through the square, the third will be as the first, on the intersection. To complete the ground, place a dot in the centre of each oblong thus formed. The foot hole is placed just above the line in the corner of the second square from the first row of ground. The catch pin is placed between, just below the line in the top right corner of the square next to the first ground row. The top of the diagram will be the top of the parchment. As the arrangement of the

Top of parchment

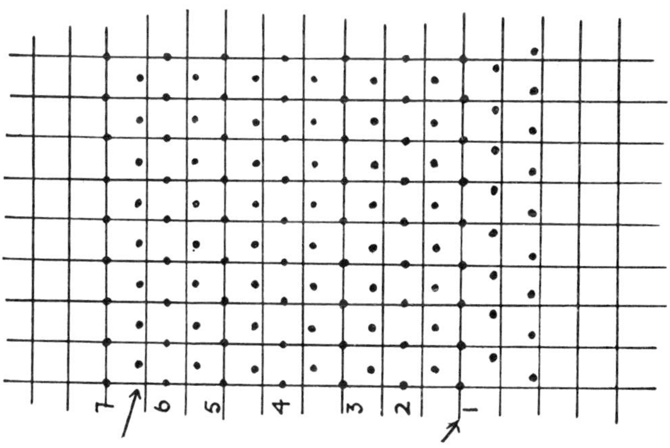

Intermediate holes inserted last

Begin to mark ground

foot prevents the parchment being used upside down, insertions should be marked which end to begin.

For *Honeycomb ground* miss out every alternate dot in every alternate row.

For *French ground* leave 2 squares between each initial row. The intermediate dots will then come on the line instead of in spaces.

In pricking some of the narrow edgings the rows of holes are usually placed closer together towards the head of the lace in order to get a less pointed effect in the geometric forms which characterise them. The simple fan pattern would be too long and pointed to look well if drawn on the net as it stands. In floral designs the necessity for altering the ground does not arise, so the change is only seen in the very simple edgings, or occasionally in fillings for wider laces where regular shapes are required.

The illustrations of ground pricking shown in some of the diagrams will suggest how the pattern can be designed on the ground. A line is drawn to represent a gimp which outlines a pattern. A pattern can be formed by just working a gimp into the ground. Alternatively the space may be either honeycomb or cloth stitch. If honeycomb, erase the alternate holes in alternate rows. For cloth stitch, except for geometric patterns, it is necessary to add holes in addition to those supplied by the ground pricking inside the pattern outline. Rub out all dots in the space and add more inside the gimp line, spaced with the width of one space or less between them.

A row of holes is required for the headpins; they should be placed about the width of one square apart a little way from the edge of the pattern. Sufficient space is needed between the headpins and pattern to allow a gimp and one or two pairs to lie smoothly. The line may follow the line of the pattern in a floral pattern, or be arranged in regular points or scallops in a geometric pattern.

TO WIND BOBBINS AND SET IN A PATTERN

THE English fashion of winding bobbins is to turn the thread away with the right hand. If a bobbin winder is used, start the thread in this way, then fix the bobbin in the machine, hold the thread in the left hand, and let it run through the hand on to the bobbin while the handle is turned with the right hand. On the Continent bobbins are usually wound in the opposite direction.

When full break the thread, and fix the loose end on to the bobbin with a *half hitch;* put the first finger of the right hand *under* the thread pointing the finger *away:* and holding the end of the thread with the bobbin in the left hand. Turn the finger to the left so that the thread forms a loop. Slip this loop over the head of the bobbin and pass the thread 3 times round it before pulling it tight. If the hitch lies on the thread and not on a head of the bobbin, these 3 turns are not necessary. When the bobbin is correctly hitched, the thread appears with the loop on top (Fig. 1) the thread in each case pulling out behind the loop. Stick a pin in the pillow at the beginning of the parchment and attach the bobbin with a *clove hitch* as follows:

Hold the bobbin by the thread in the left hand, put the first finger of the right hand under the thread pointing away, and make the turn as before. Twist the loose end of the thread round the pin moving from front on left, round behind pin to right, and then slip the loop over the pin without turning or twisting it (Fig. 2). Hang as many bobbins as liked on one pin and then stick another near and hang on more until the required number is reached.

Loop for half hitch

Fig. 1

Loop on bobbin & loop over pin

Fig. 2

Foundation Stitch or Whole Stitch

The stitch is made by 2 couples and consists of 3 stages, 1 bobbin moved to the right, 2 to the left, and 1 to the right. Number the bobbins, 1, 2, 3, 4 (Fig. 3). Lift 2 and lay it over 3.

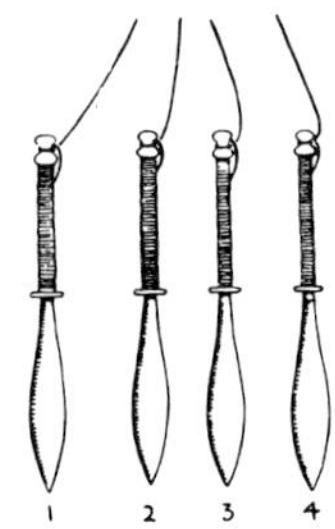

Fig. 3 Bobbins ready for stitch

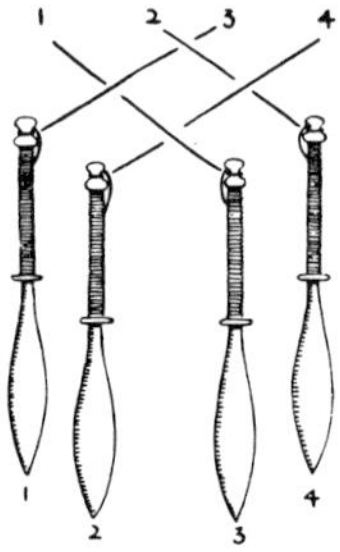

Stitch made *Fig. 4*

Then take 4 in the right hand and 2 (previously 3) in the left and move them simultaneously to the left so that 4 lies over 3 and 2 lies over 1. Now place 2 over 3 (Fig. 4).

The first 2 stages make a *half stitch*.

The stitch is the same in every position or in whatever direction the work is being done. It may be followed by *twists* which are always made in the same direction. A twist means putting the right hand bobbin of a pair over the left hand bobbin. Always look at the threads, not the bobbins, to make sure that they are not improperly crossed or displaced, before making a stitch.

When a number of whole stitches follow after one another without twists, a piece of *clothwork* is formed (Fig. 5). At the end of each row a pin is usually stuck to hold the working couple in position. This couple is the pair which starts the row and comes right through—the other pairs are sometimes called passives.

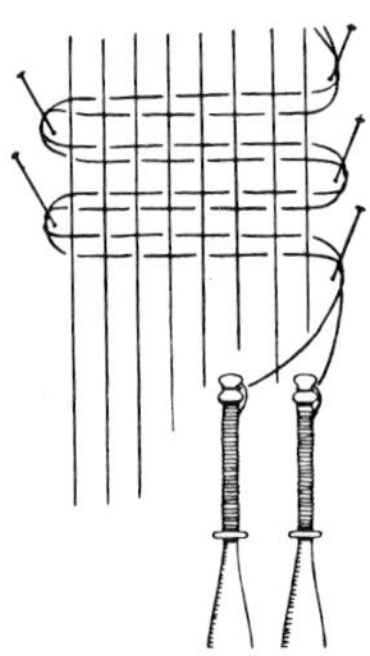

Fig. 5 Whole stitch

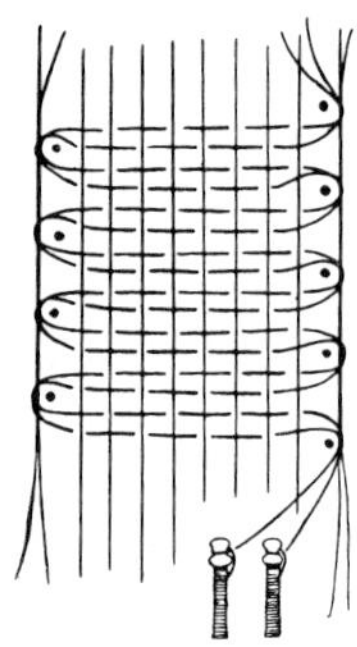

A footing *Fig. 6*

The foot is the straight edge which is sewn to a garment. By English lacemakers the parchment is always pinned with the head to the left. Any part of the pattern which is not ground, foot or head, is usually termed by lacemakers a "bud". These various buds and ground are best studied in connection with the patterns where they occur.

A beginner may prick 2 rows of holes and practise whole stitch if desired before beginning a pattern. An outside pair may be added on each side to form a "footing" (Fig. 6). Each time *before* working the outside pair, twist the working pair 3 times. *After* working the outside pair, twist both outer pairs 3 times, then stick the pin under the 2 twisted pairs and *not* between them. The outer pair now remains outside, ready twisted, and the inner pair works back through the other bobbins.

It is advisable to keep a good row of pins (about 2″) along the footside. The rest of the pattern needs plenty of pins to prevent the threads drawing up and getting displaced. When sufficient pins have been stuck, remove those from behind to use in front, taking care not to remove too many from the foot.

The hands while working should be kept downwards, as when playing the piano. The knuckles are often used to keep the bobbins in place when there are a large number. Bobbins may be lifted to facilitate the sticking of a pin, but should always be laid down again in their proper place, so that the order of the threads is not changed. Any bobbins not in use should be pushed to one side or at the back of the pillow as far as possible in the correct order. The bobbins in use should be in the space in front of the worker.

There should be about 3″ thread between the head of the bobbins and pins and all threads must be of an even length to avoid getting out of order. The length of thread unwound does, however, depend to some extent on the shape and size of the pillow.

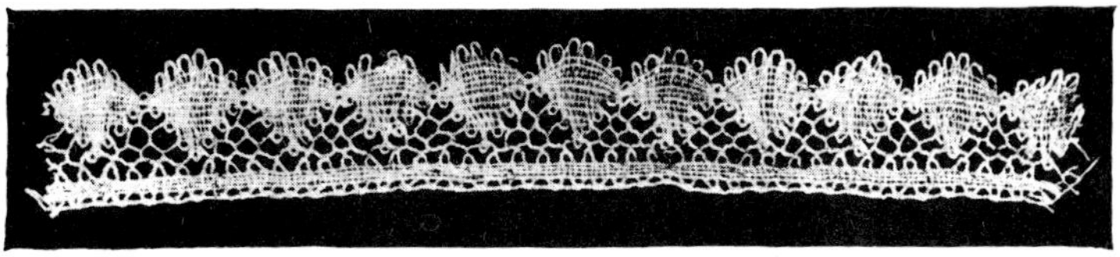

POINT GROUND FAN PATTERN

THIS pattern is simple and attractive, The fan, consisting of cloth work, may be worked first and completely finished before the ground need be done.

Eleven pairs of bobbins are required.

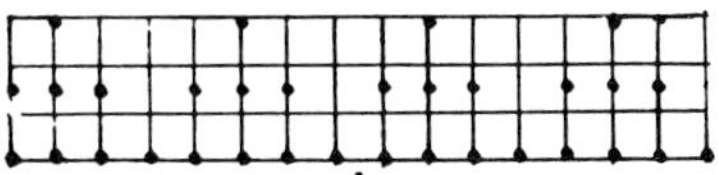

1

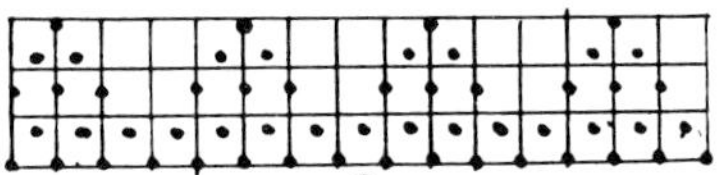

2

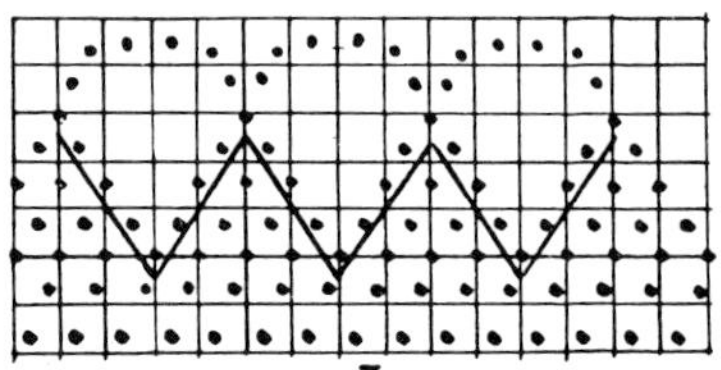

3

The Fan

1. Begin with 4 couples, stick the first pin in the hole which comes between the 2 fans (A), leaving 1 couple to the left of the pin. This couple is the working couple. Work 3 whole stitches to the right, using each of the 3 pairs with the workers, twist the workers twice, right over left, and stick a pin under it in the first hole on the right (B). Work 3 whole stitches to the left, twist the workers twice, and stick the pin under them in the first hole on the left, i.e. on the outer edge of the fan (C).
2. Work 4 stitches to the right, taking in a new pair, twist and stick a pin as before in the next hole on the right. Work 4 stitches to the left, stick a pin in the next hole on the outer edge.
3. Proceed in this way, taking in a new couple every time on the right until the point at the foot of the fan has been reached, (D). 6 stitches will now have been worked.
4. The fan now gets smaller. On the next row to the right work 5 stitches, thus working 1 pair less on each row. The last pin will be stuck in the hole beginning the next fan (E).

The workers will be to the left of the pin. Twist each of the 4 pairs left out of the fan twice before working the ground.

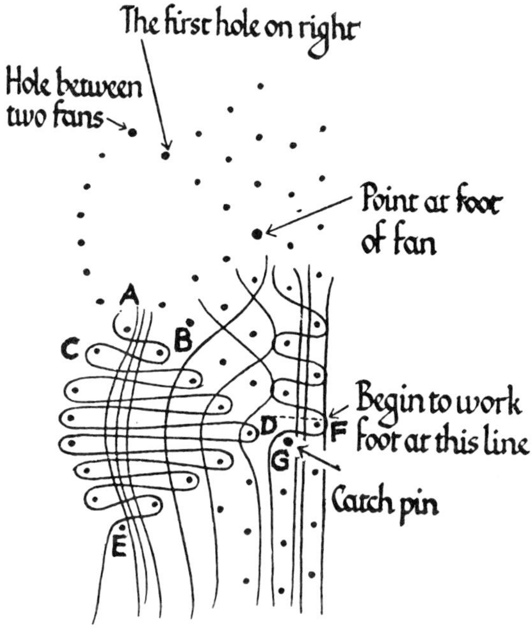

The lower fan shows the position of the eleven couples when the pattern is worked. Each line represents a pair of bobbins. The diagram shows first row of ground not worked, as when beginning the lace.

The Ground

Bucks lacemakers often call the ground stitch "half stitch" and talk of half stitch laces, meaning point ground lace.

To work the *ground stitch* use 2 pairs of bobbins. Work a half stitch and twist each pair twice. Stick a pin between the pairs and leave uncovered.

Foot and Ground

Count from the right the footside, 4 couples and take the fourth pair as workers. Work 2 whole stitches to the right, twist the workers 3 times, work a whole stitch with the remaining pair and twist both pairs 3 times. Stick the footpin under the 2 pairs at F. The inner of the 2 pairs is now used to work 2 whole stitches to the left. Twist this pair 3 times and stick a pin under it at the next hole on the left (G). This pin is called the *catchpin.* After the catchpin always follow with the catchpin stitch which joins the ground to the foot. Work a ground stitch with the next pair from the left (this comes out of the point of the fan) but do not stick a pin. Leave the right-hand pair, use the left pair and the next from the left and work another ground stitch with a pin stuck between them at the next hole to the left. Repeat twice more. Begin the foot again with the fourth pair from the right, and work in the same way but only 2 ground stitch pins will be stuck. Then work the foot again and only 1 pin in the ground, then the foot again, finishing with the catchpin stitch.

The pattern is now complete. Begin the next fan as before, using the workers on the left and working 3 whole stitches through the first 3 pairs to the right.

Note

1. The pattern can be worked with a gimp if liked, in which case, the gimp is passed from the right to the left under one bobbin and over the next through the 4 pairs which come out of the fan. After finishing the ground the gimp is passed through the 4 pairs from the ground. After passing a gimp through, always twist each pair twice.

2. The 2 pairs belonging to the fan which do not come into the ground are not twisted and the 2 which run straight down through the foot are never twisted.

3. The workers are always twisted before the pin is stuck, but never after.

4. Many lacemakers make the outside stitch in the foot of the point ground lace a half stitch instead of a whole stitch. This counteracts the tendency for the foot to become too tight.

5. The foot pins should be slanting outwards towards the right to keep the line straight. All other pins should be stuck slightly backwards.

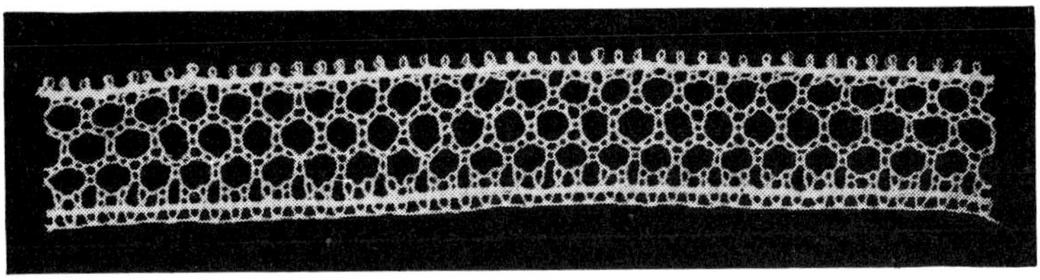

HONEYCOMB GROUND EDGING

The pricking is similar to the point ground, but in every alternate row each alternate hole is omitted.

Thirteen pairs of bobbins are required.

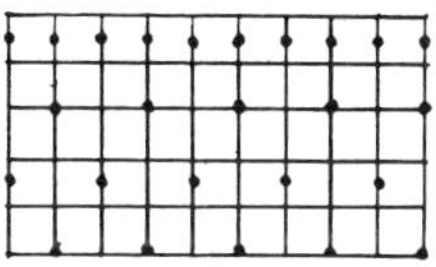

1

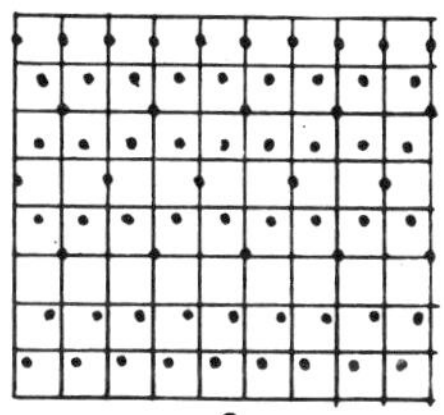

2

Honeycomb Stitch

Using 2 pairs of bobbins, work a half stitch, twist both pairs once and stick a pin between them. Cover the pin by working another half stitch and twist with the same bobbins. This honeycomb stitch is similar to the point ground except that the pairs are twisted once instead of twice and the pin is covered with a second stitch instead of being left open.

The edging shown consists of honeycomb ground with foot attached on the one side and headpins, being pearls or picots, on the right. Honeycomb filling is frequently surrounded by a gimp. This method will be made clear in other patterns.

When working the ground, the row which has all holes complete can be called a *long row* while the alternate row may be called a *short row*.

1. Begin with the first long row A-X, A being the outside foot pin. Work the foot as for the point ground but at the

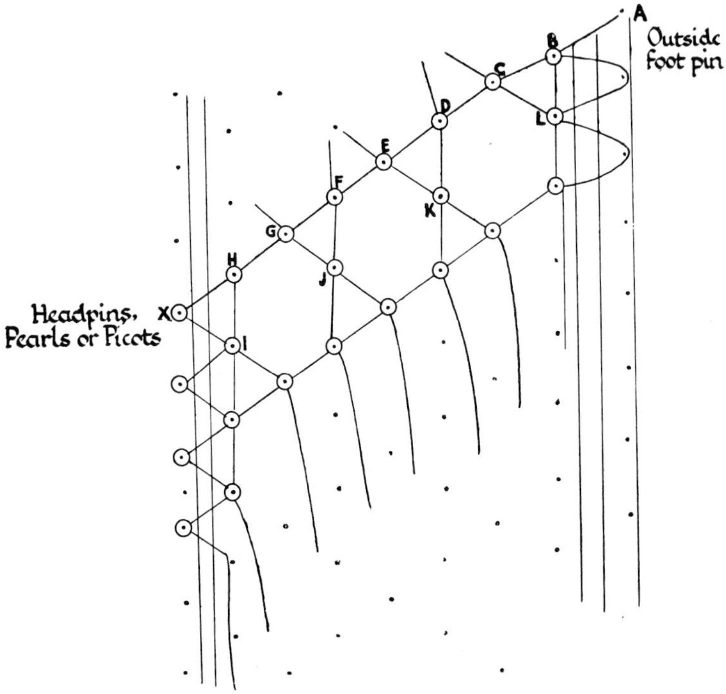

Each line represents a pair of bobbins.

catchpin B (second hole diagonally from A), work a honeycomb stitch with a new pair. Leave the right pair, use the left pair with a new pair from the left and work a honeycomb stitch at the next hole diagonally to the left (C). Repeat honeycomb stitches at each of the next 5 holes, D, E, F, G and H.

2. *Heading.* Use the left pair from the last honeycomb stitch as workers. Work 2 whole stitches through the 2 passive pairs, and use the workers to make the headpin.

3. *Headpin—Pearl or Picot.* Twist 5 times for a fine thread and 3 times for a coarser, putting the right hand bobbin over the left bobbin as it lies on the pillow. Then lift the outside bobbin on the left, put the pin on top of the thread and bring the thread round the pin. Then stick the pin. Hold that bobbin still in the left hand, and with the right hand pick up the other bobbin

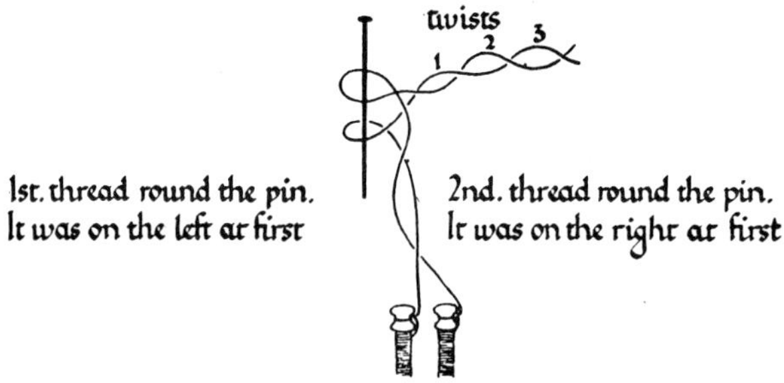

and pass that thread round the pin, moving it out to the left, up and around the pin. Twist the pair three times or twice according to the thickness of the thread.

4. Use the pair which made the headpin as workers and work 2 whole stitches to the right ready for working the short row I, J, K, and L. At the first hole I, make a honeycomb stitch with the pair used for the headpin and the pair hanging from H on the previous row. The left-hand pair may be worked to the left to make a headpin as before, then 2 whole stitches to the right through the passives to leave hanging for the next long row.

5. At the next hole J, use pairs hanging from the previous row G and F. When the pin is covered there will be 2 pairs hanging from the pin. Make another honeycomb stitch at K in a similar manner. The next hole is the catchpin, therefore work the foot as before, using the fourth pair from the right; now work the honeycomb stitch at L, the catchpin. Again use the fourth pair from the right to work the foot and then work another long row followed by a short row.

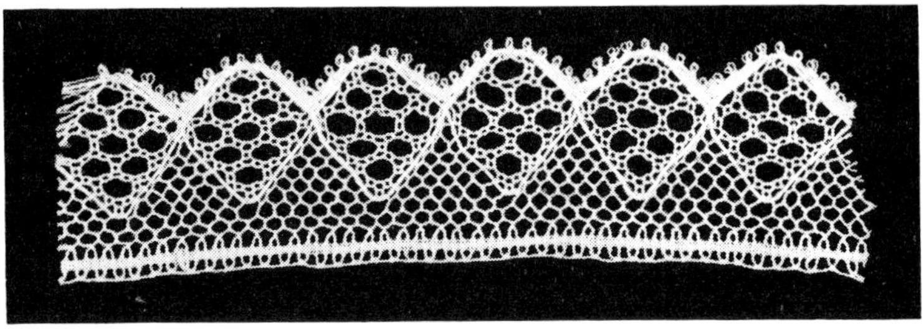

HONEYCOMB FAN

Twenty pairs of bobbins and two gimp bobbins are required.

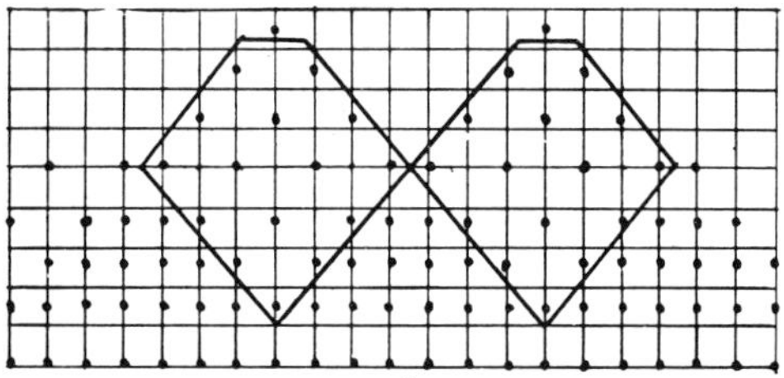

1

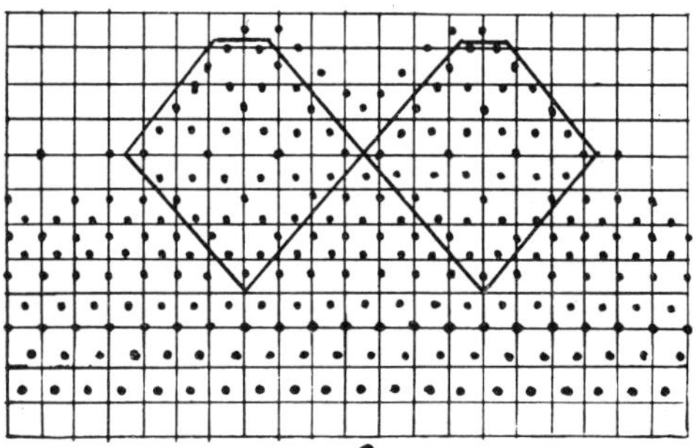

2

1. Work the foot and ground between the fans as for the small fan.

2. *The Fan.* Thread one gimp from left to right through 7 pairs coming from the ground. Thread the second gimp from right to left through 6 pairs from the head. There will be one pair outside the gimp. Begin the honeycomb at the top corner hole, A, using the first pair from each gimp. Work a "long

row" as for the honeycomb edging from right to left. Pass the gimp through the last pair, work 1 whole stitch with the pair outside the gimp and work a headpin as for the honeycomb edging. Work 1 whole stitch to the right, pass the gimp between the 2 bobbins and work a "short row" to the right.

Continue the honeycomb filling till all rows are completed. The first row is the only one where a headpin is worked and there will be one pair hanging from the end pin of every row.

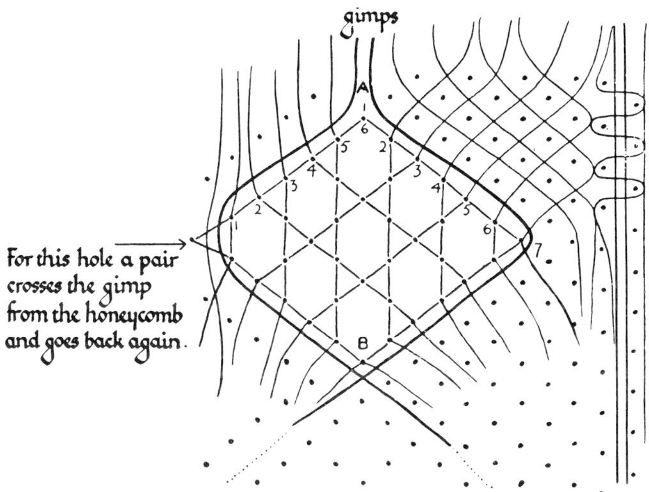

Thread the gimps through the pairs on each side and cross between the last 2 pairs from the lower corner, B.

3. *The Heading.* The headpins are pearls worked from the top of one scallop to the next.

Begin with the first pair from the gimp, i.e. the pair hanging from the end of the first short row. Work 1 whole stitch to the left, work a headpin in the first hole and work 1 whole stitch to the right. Take the second pair from the gimp, work 2 whole stitches to the left, headpin in the second hole, and 1 whole stitch to the right. Use the third pair from the gimp, work 3 whole stitches to the left, headpin and 1 whole stitch to the

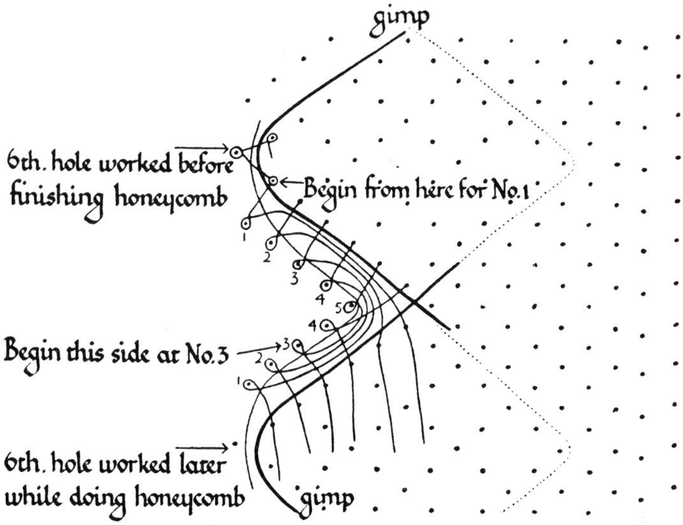

The dotted line indicates gimp as marked on the parchment

right. Repeat similarly with the fourth and fifth pairs from the gimp. The lowest point of the slope will now have been worked. The sixth and last pair from the gimp is worked through 6 pairs to the left, then a headpin at the first hole of the second slope and 4 whole stitches to the right.

Now reverse the order. Begin at the left, at the outside. Work 1 whole stitch with the 2 outside pairs, work headpin and 3 whole stitches to the right. Return to the outside edge, work 1 whole stitch, headpin and 2 whole stitches to the right. The last headpin is worked in a similar manner, finishing with 1 whole stitch to the right.

Pass the gimp from the right-hand side of the fan through 6 pairs from the head, again leaving 1 pair outside the gimp.

This system of working the headpins can be applied to other point ground patterns.

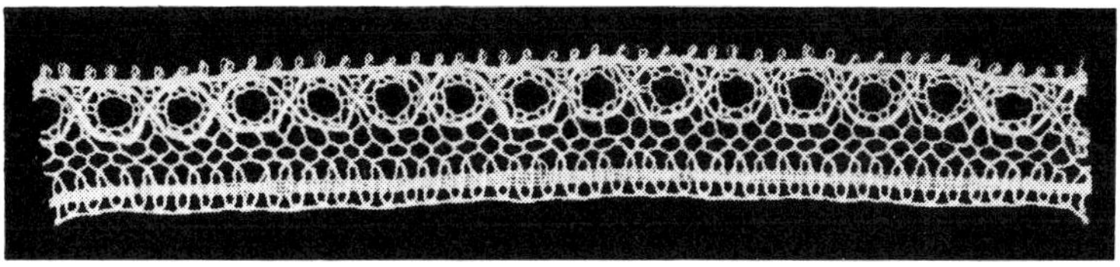

SINGLE RING OR PEA PATTERN

This pattern introduces a honeycomb ring which is common to many point ground patterns.

Twelve pairs of bobbins and two gimps are required.

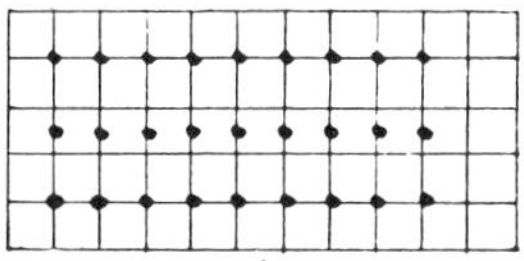

1

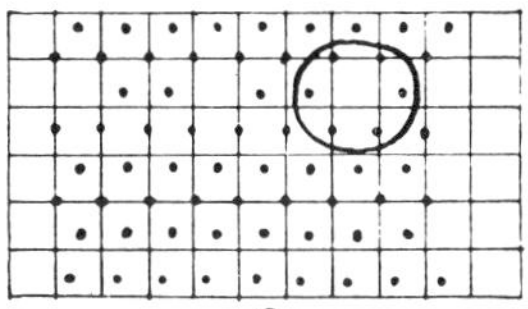

2

1. Work the foot and ground to complete as many holes as possible outside the ring. Naming the 3 ground holes encircling the ring X, Y and Z, it will be seen that X and Y can be worked and the rows will slope diagonally with these holes. Z cannot be worked at this stage.

2. *The Ring.* The ring enclosed by a gimp thread, consists of 6 holes, one each at top and bottom, A and F respectively, and 2 on each side, B and C on the right, and D and E on the left. Thread 1 gimp thread to the right through 2 pairs from the ground holes X and Y. Thread the second gimp to the left through 2 new pairs. Twist each pair twice.

Begin with 1 pair from each gimp, i.e. the 2 middle pairs. Work a honeycomb stitch at A. Leave the left pair; use the right pair to work a honeycomb stitch with the next pair from the right at B. The pair on the right is required to work the ground stitch Z, outside the ring. Pass the gimp between the 2 bobbins, twist twice, and work the ground stitch. Bring the pair back into the ring by passing the gimp between the 2 bobbins. Twist twice and work the third honeycomb stitch

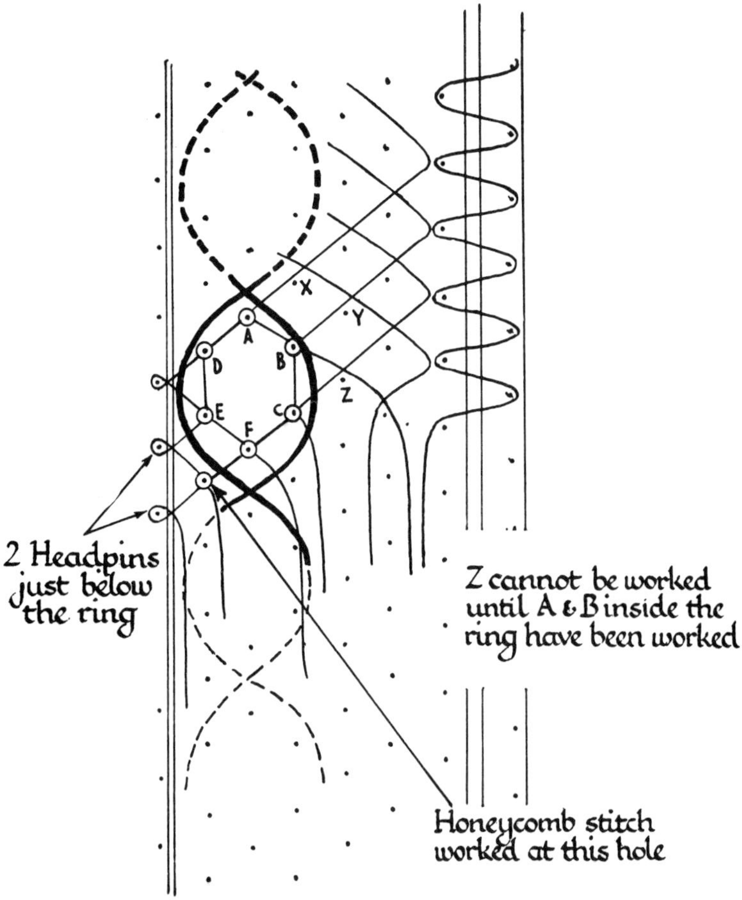

Each line represents a pair of bobbins except in the case of the gimps. Dotted line shows where the gimp is marked on the parchment.

at C. Leave both pairs and work the left side of the ring. Use the left pair from A and a new pair from the gimp and work a honeycomb stitch at D. The left pair is used to work a headpin just outside the ring between D and E. Pass the gimp between the bobbins. Use the pair as workers and work 2 whole stitches to the left through 2 pairs of passives. Work the headpin, as for honeycomb edging.

Work 2 whole stitches to the right, pass the gimp between the bobbins, twist twice and work the third honeycomb stitch on the left at E. Using the pair on the right with the next pair on the right, work another honeycomb stitch at F to complete the ring. Thread each gimp through 2 pairs and cross at the bottom of the ring. Twist each pair twice.

Headpins just below the ring

Begin with the first pair from the ring (hanging from E), work 2 whole stitches to the left, a headpin and 2 whole stitches to the right. Twist twice and work a honeycomb stitch at the hole between the 2 rings with the next pair from the ring (from F). Use the left pair to work 2 whole stitches to the left, work a second headpin and 2 whole stitches back to the right. Thread the gimp coming from the right of the previous ring through 2 pairs in readiness for the next ring.

Work more ground so that the second gimp can be threaded through 2 pairs from the ground and proceed as before.

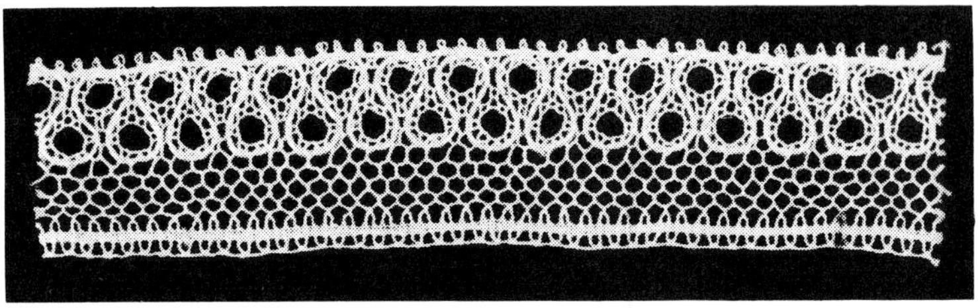

DOUBLE RING PATTERN

Seventeen pairs of bobbins and one gimp bobbin are required.

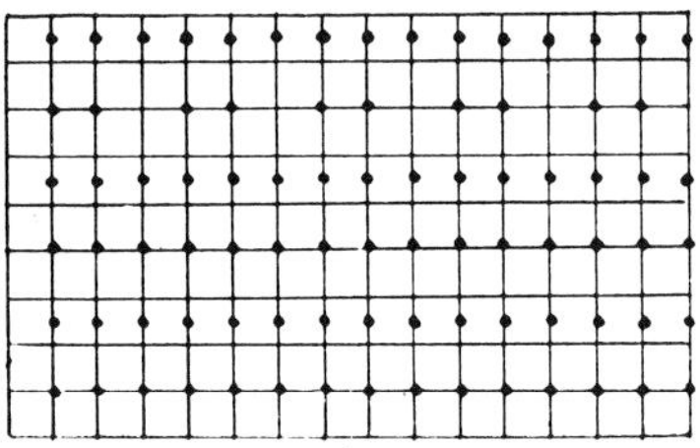

1

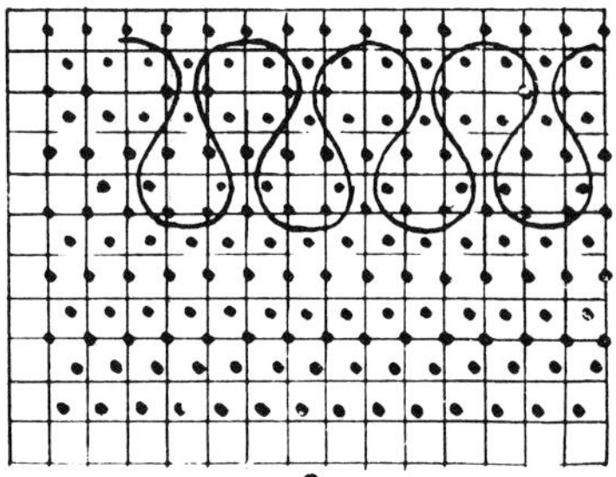

2

WORK the foot and ground as for the single ring, working the ground holes X and Y encircling the lower ring. Pass the gimp through 3 new pairs from the left and then continue to the right through the 2 pairs coming from behind the holes X and Y.

Begin with the 2 centre pairs—one new pair and one from the ground, and work the right side of the ring as for the single ring pattern.

Left side

The ring is pear shaped so it will be noticed that there are 3 honeycomb holes to be worked on the left side. Work the third hole as the second. Leave the pair on the left, use the right pair with the pair coming from the second hole and work a honeycomb stitch at the hole below the third and second. Complete the ring as for the single ring.

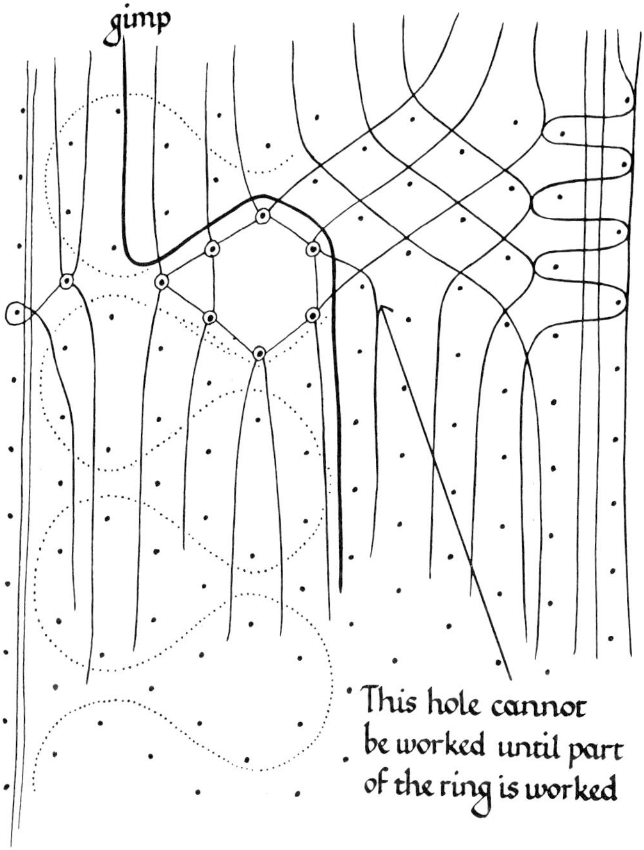

The dotted line indicates the gimp as marked on the parchment.

Thread the gimp to the left through the 5 pairs from the ring and 2 new pairs. This time the pointed end is on the right and is worked as for the previous ring. The left side, near the head is worked as for the left side of the single ring. When complete, thread the gimp to the right through the 5 pairs from the ring.

Work the 2 headpins and hole between the left-hand rings, then the foot and ground ready for the next right-hand ring.

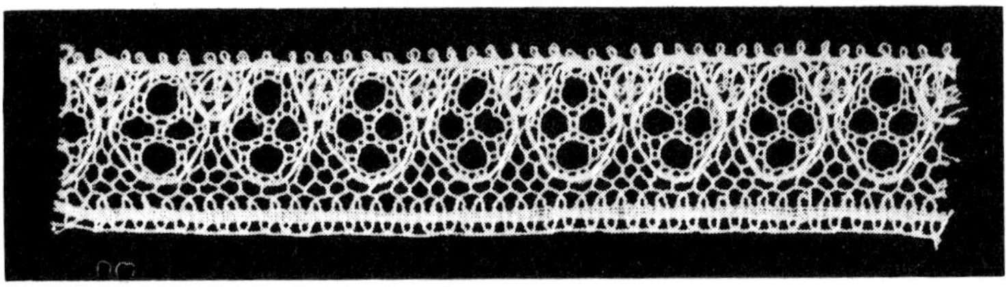

CAT'S FACE

A PATTERN with this type of honeycomb bud is often called, by the lacemakers, "cat's face".

Fifteen pairs of bobbins and two gimp bobbins are required.

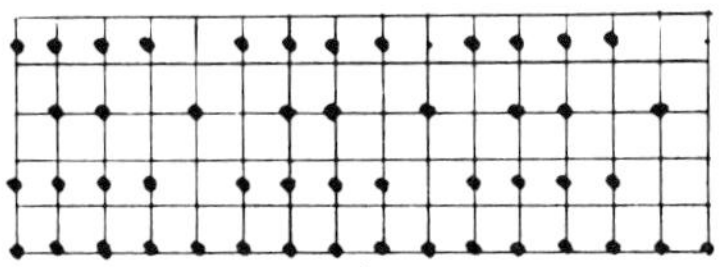

1

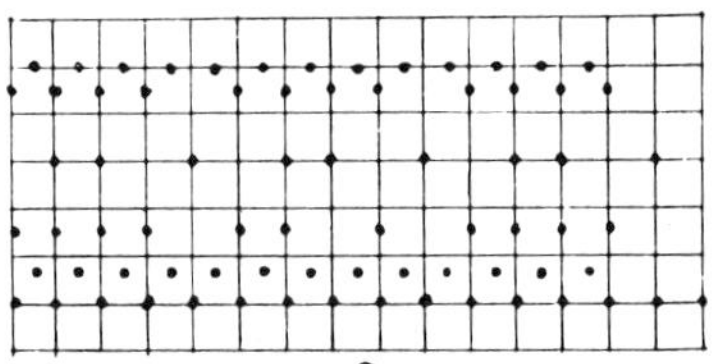

2

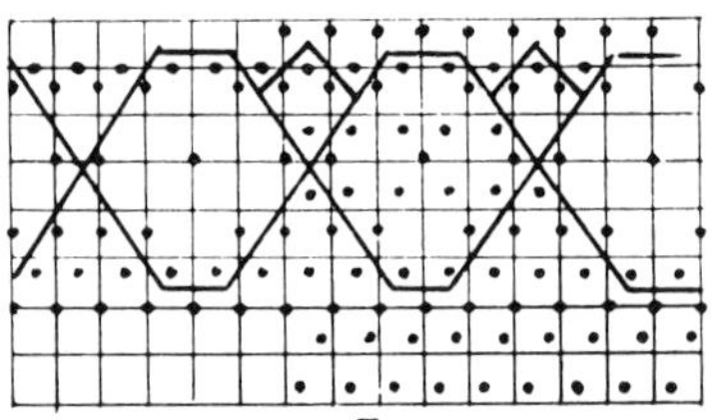

3

1. Begin by working the foot and rows of ground above the honeycomb bud.

2. Work the square bud on the head side in whole stitch or cloth stitch. Begin at the top corner with 2 pairs, stick and

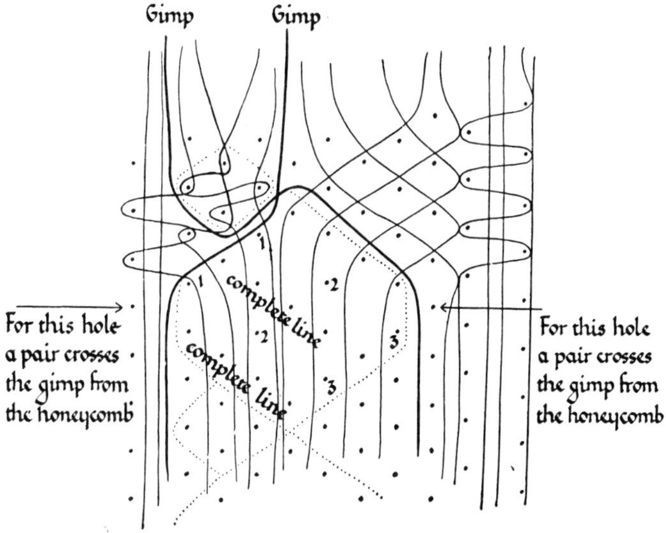

Each line represents a pair of bobbins except in the case of gimps. Dotted line shows where the gimp is marked on the parchment.

cover the pin. Use the left pair as workers, take in a pair from the left at the hole on the left. Work back to the right through 2 pairs and take in a new pair. Work to the left, through 2 pairs, leaving out a pair at the corner, and stick a pin in the lower hole, finishing the square. Cover the pin. There are now 4 pairs hanging from the ground, and 2 pairs from each side of the bud.

3. *Working the gimps.* Place 1 gimp in between the 2 sets of bobbins and the other to the left of the square. Bring the latter through all 4 pairs from the bud, cross the middle gimp and then through 4 pairs from the ground. Pass the other gimp to the left through 2 pairs from the square. Twist each pair twice.

4. Work the 2 headpins coming just below the square bud, using the same method as in the Ring pattern. Bring the left-hand gimp through 2 more pairs and there will be 8 pairs ready for working the honeycomb, 4 on one side and 4 on the other.

5. *Honeycomb filling.* Begin at the top hole with one pair from each side, work a long row to the right, 4 holes being worked. Pass the gimp through the workers and work the ground hole outside the gimp. Pass the gimp back through the workers, bringing them again into the honeycomb ground. Work 1 short row, then a long row and another short row. Before working the last long row, thread the gimp through the last pair to work the headpin. Work 2 whole stitches through the passives, work the headpin and 2 whole stitches to the right, thread the gimp between the 2 bobbins and work the long row.

6. Bring each gimp through 4 pairs to cross at the bottom. Continue the right gimp through 2 more pairs on the left. The remaining 2 from the honeycomb ground are used to work the 2 headpins and honeycomb stitch. Carry the gimp on, through one pair from the single hole, and one pair from the last headpin. Repeat the pattern.

WIDE HONEYCOMB PATTERN

THIS pattern is one which can successfully be enlarged to be worked in 100 linen thread. It is simple enough for the worker to "set in" the pattern without a definite number of bobbins being stated.

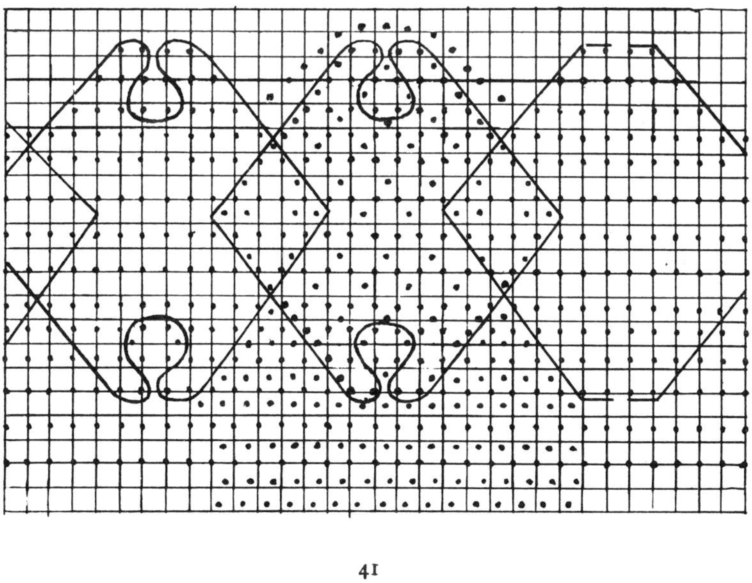

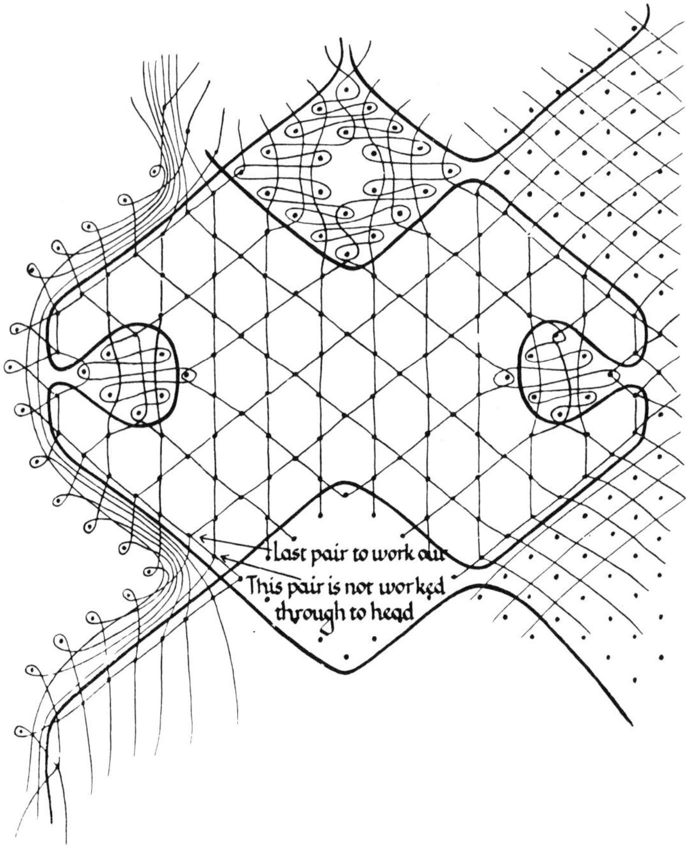

In working head pins in this pattern note that the last pair from the honeycomb is not used for a headpin at all. The pair before takes you one hole into the next head.

A new feature, which occurs in many laces, is the hole in the middle of the piece of cloth work. Begin the pattern at this point.

Start at the top hole with 1 pair from each side, and work the cloth stitch, taking in a new pair at each hole till the 3 pins, including the top one, have been stuck on each side. There will now be 6 pairs, including the workers. Work back through 3 pairs, stick the pin in the centre hole and cover the pin. The left pair will now become workers for the left side, while the pair on the right will be workers for the right. Continue the cloth stitch on each side, taking in new pairs and leaving them out at the appropriate places till the 2 workers meet at the bottom hole. Work a whole stitch with the 2 workers, stick in the pin and continue the cloth stitch to finish the bud.

The following hints will be found helpful in continuing the pattern:

1. The little round buds at each end of the honeycomb ground are worked in cloth stitch. The gimp is passed through 5 pairs from the honeycomb filling. In the middle of the rounded side, the gimp must be passed through the worker in order to finish the row of honeycomb which comes down the middle of the bud. After working the honeycomb stitch, pass the gimp through the worker and continue the cloth work.

2. In the first row of honeycomb on the foot side, the gimp must be passed through a pair from the filling to work a ground stitch. The pair is then brought back into the ground to finish the next row of honeycomb. The same thing occurs before starting the honeycomb after the bud has been worked.

3. The heading is worked as for the honeycomb fan, but the 3 holes at the top of the scallop are each worked by passing the worker out from the honeycomb filling and back again to continue the filling.

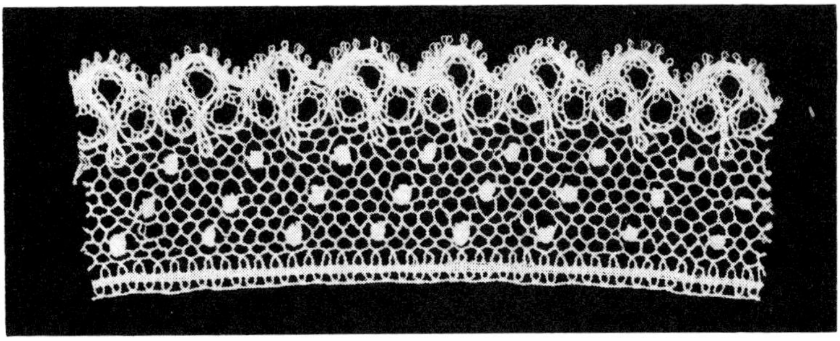

TRUE LOVER'S KNOT or HOOK AND EYE

THIS pattern may be worked as a narrow edging or with a deeper band of ground, as preferred.

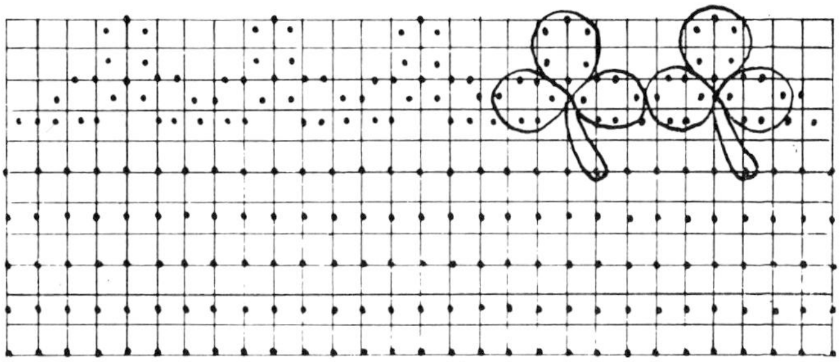

1

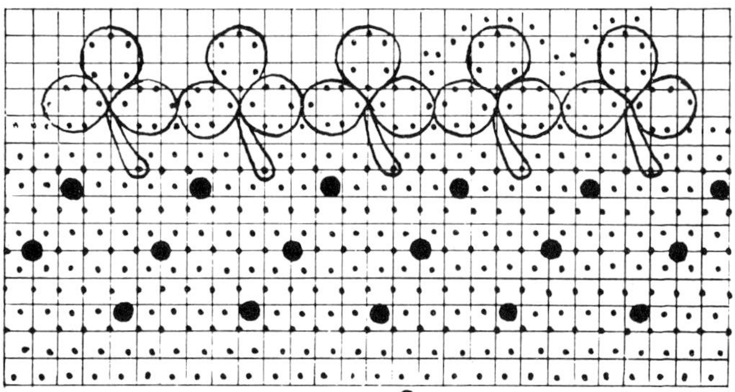

2

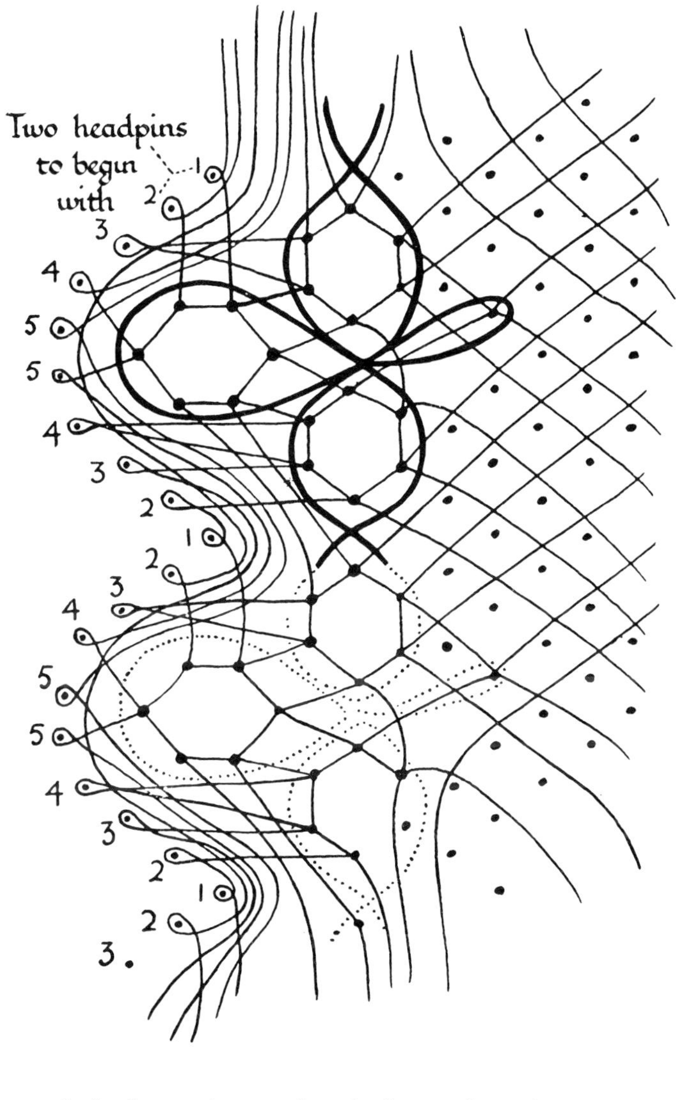

Work the foot and ground ready for working the first ring of the trefoil as for the single ring. Before beginning the trefoil, the headpins below the preceding bud will already have been worked, and one starting up the next slope outwards. There are 10 holes encircling each trefoil, Nos. 1–5 up one side and Nos. 5–1 down the other, No. 1 belonging to both trefoils.

1. Work the first ring as for the single ring, working headpin No. 3 on the headpin side of the ring.

2. *Head.* Work 1 whole stitch with the 2 outside pairs, work headpin No. 4 and 2 whole stitches to the right. Work No. 5 in a similar manner with 1 whole stitch to the right (compare honeycomb fan).

3. *Outer ring.* Bring the gimp coming from the right of the first ring through 5 pairs to the left (2 from the first ring, 2 from the head and 1 from No. 4 headpin). The outer ring is irregular as it starts with 2 holes side by side. Work the first on the right using 1 pair from the first ring and one from the head. The right pair is used to work the next hole on the right. The left one is used to work the next parallel hole on the left. Then work the hole in the apex of the trefoil, and then the 2 lower ones, left to right to complete the ring. Make sure the ground is worked up to the stem.

4. *Stem of trefoil.* Bring the gimp to the right through 5 pairs, cross the other gimp and through 4 to make the stem. Work a honeycomb stitch at the hole in the stem with the 2 pairs lying ready for it. Use the left pair to work 2 whole stitches to the left. Bring the gimp back to the left through 4 pairs, cross the other gimp and bring that gimp through 2 pairs back to the right. The left-hand gimp which has formed the stem is passed through 2 more pairs from the outer ring ready to begin the last ring.

5. *Heading.* Work the second No. 5 headpin by bringing the third pair from the left through the 2 outside pairs and 1 stitch back to the right.

6. *Last ring.* Work the ground down to the ring and then work as for the first ring. No. 4 headpin will be worked on the headside of the ring. Finish the ring and return to:

7. *Headside.* Work No. 3 and 2 headpins using the pairs from the ring as for the honeycomb fan. Work No. 1 with the outer pair and 4 whole stitches to the right. Work No. 2 with the outermost couple and 3 stitches to the right.

Square Plaits

In this pattern the ground is diversified with square plaits or tallies. No pin need be stuck, so instead of the hole is a blank spot, which may be blackened. Where this occurs the plait is made using the 2 pairs which have been used for the ground stitch. Make a square plait as follows:

Use the second bobbin from the left. Make slightly longer and weave it over the third, under the fourth, back over the fourth, under the third, over the first, back under the first, and so on till large enough to fill the hole. Only 1 bobbin is moving; the others should be allowed to lie on the pillow. The travelling bobbin must be kept slack while the other 3 are pulled down firmly. When drawing the travelling bobbin up to make a good shape, pull the 2 outer bobbins outwards. The thread of the traveller should finish on the left and finally be twisted round No. 1 bobbin 3 times. Twist the other 2 bobbins 3 times and proceed with the ground.

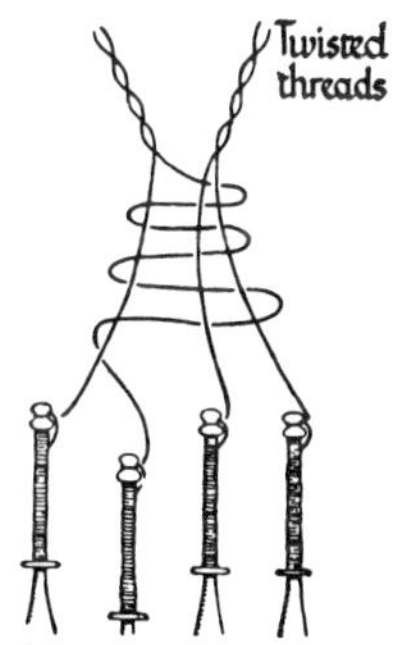

A plait in the making

A FINE OLD BUCKS PATTERN

Thirty-two pairs of bobbins and two gimps are required. It is an interesting example of the semi-geometrical type. The variation in the alternate heads produces a delightful effect, and the heavy and light parts are wonderfully balanced and contrasted, without rendering the work over complicated. It is a masterpiece in the art of obtaining a pleasant effect while keeping the work simple. (For pricking see page 60.)

Cloth work bud with open centre

This has 7 holes on the left upper side, the right-hand side being indented with a gimp. Begin at the top with 2 couples, as for ordinary cloth diamond with a gimp on each side. Work first to the left, take in a couple, stick up and cover the pin, then to the right, take in a couple, stick up and cover the pin, back to the left, take in another couple, stick up and cover the pin. Work to the right again, but this time *leave out* 2 couples. The next process is working a *nookpin*. Before sticking up, bring the gimp from the right through the 2 pairs left out, then through the worker, stick the pin under the worker and take the gimp back through it and through the next 2 pairs and 2 more pairs from the ground. Work to the left to No. 4 pin and back towards the right. The second lobe contains 3 holes, the first upper is slightly above the last nookpin so is worked separately with a fresh pair from the ground and one pair from the upper lobe. Stick the pin and cover. Continue the cloth work with the original worker to the further hole. Work back to the left to No. 5 hole, after which the bobbins are divided for the hole in the middle of the bud.

Work through 3 pairs, stick up at the top of the opening, cover the pin, work to the left and finish the left side as for the wide honeycomb pattern.

Right side

Use the pair left from the top hole of opening as workers, work to the right, leave out 1 pair, and stick up in the third hole of the second lobe, and back to opening, then through 2 pairs to the right. Bring the gimp through 3 pairs to the left and stick up nookpin. Complete the ground holes outside the bud. Pass gimp to right through 4 pairs (2 from upper lobe and 2 pairs from the ground).

Centre lobe

The upper and lower holes are worked separately as in the second lobe. The working couple from the middle will go once through to the outer hole and back to join up at the lower hole of the opening. Work back to the right and work nook-pin beginning the fourth lobe. Continue the cloth work, and finish the bud, the worker going through to the first and second hole while the lower third hole is worked separately.

Note

If the bud is begun to the left and divided for the hole from the left, work first to the right when joining up the opening.

Head

As one cloth work bud is slightly nearer the head than the other, the left-hand point of this needs a pair taken in from the head. Headpins must be worked as directed in honeycomb fan, down to the lowest hole made with the last pair from the honeycomb. The pair nearest the gimp will be taken into the cloth work bud, and will be left out again to be used for the headpin in the next head. Work back to within 1 pair. Continue working the headpins to the top and at the apex, in and

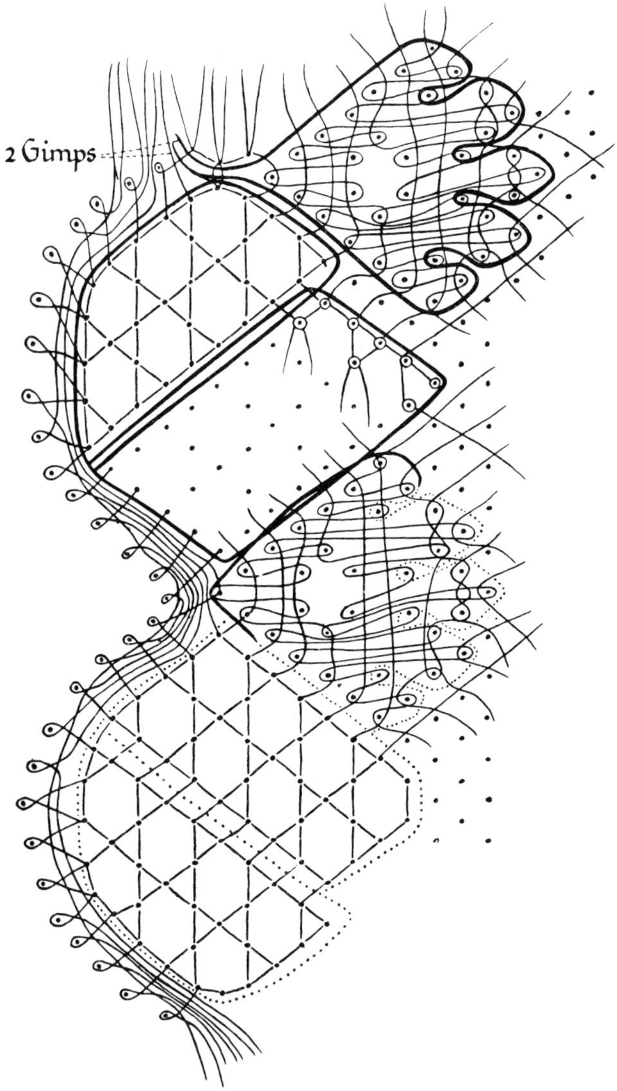
2 Gimps

out with the honeycomb filling. It is necessary to work 1 extra headpin, using the 2 pairs outside the gimp, in order to bring the headpins far enough round the curve to begin working out the lower slope after working the filling.

The honeycomb filling is in 2 sections, each surrounded by gimps which must lie crossed at one corner of the section and lie double between the 2 sections. In the next head, where the cloth work is lower down, the lowest headpin is made with the pair *before* the one from the last honeycomb hole. This pair is worked back, leaving one couple to go straight into the next honeycomb. The 2 pairs from the last honeycomb hole in the section have the 2 gimps put through them and the *same* pairs begin the honeycomb on the next head. Note that in neither head is the lowest headpin worked in the usual way.

Foot and ground are worked in the usual manner and a square plait may be added or omitted as required.

Nookpin occurs in a larger number of floral patterns so the principles used here can be applied elsewhere. The gimp is brought through part of the cloth work and met by the working couple from the opposite direction. The nookpin fixes the worker and gimp, and is covered by them, and both worker and gimp then travel in opposite directions. The cloth work must be as neat and close as possible on each side of the nook and there must be enough bobbins to leave out when the width of the bud is decreasing.

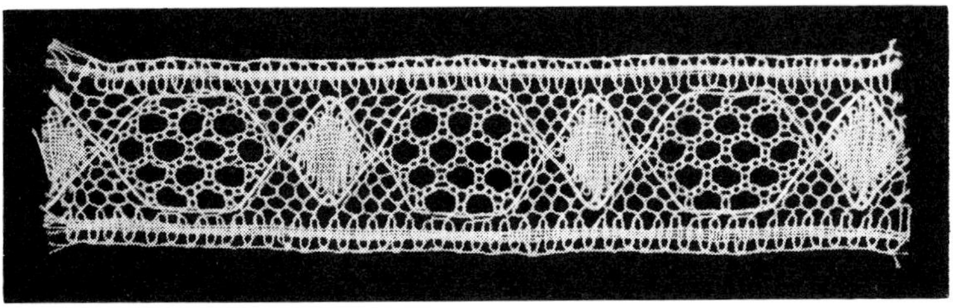

INSERTION

This insertion consists of honeycomb, cloth stitch diamond and point ground.

Eighteen pairs of bobbins and two gimps are required.

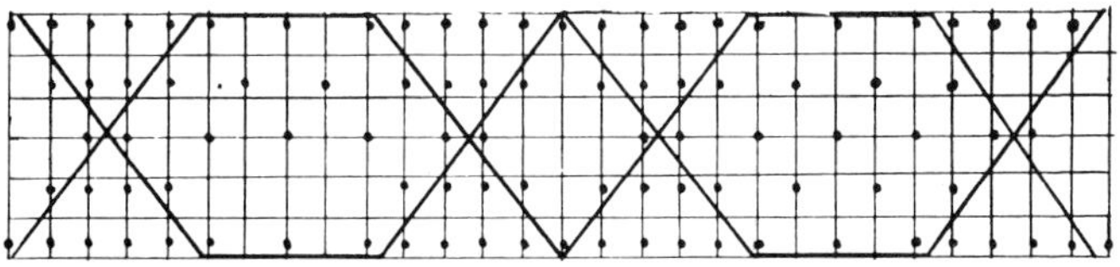

1

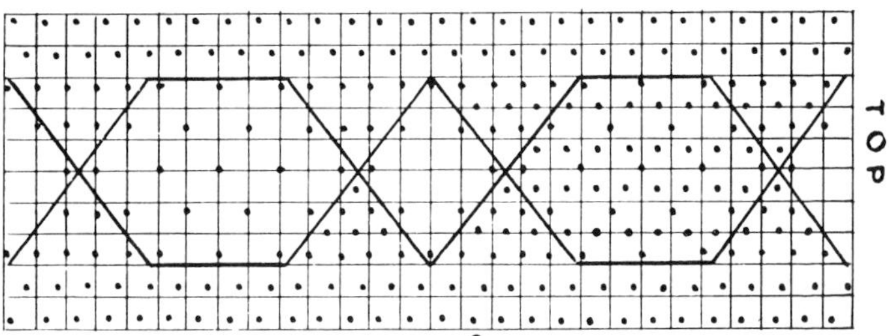

2

As no new processes are incorporated the pattern should easily be worked if the following points are noted:

1. There are 2 open spaces each side of the honeycomb bud. In each case the gimp will be passed through the outer pair and this pair will be used to work the catchpin stitch outside the gimp. The foot is worked again and another stitch worked before taking the pair back into the bud.

2. The foot in the head may be puzzling but it is only the exact reverse of the normal foot. Begin with the fourth pair from the *left* instead of the right, and work to the *left*.

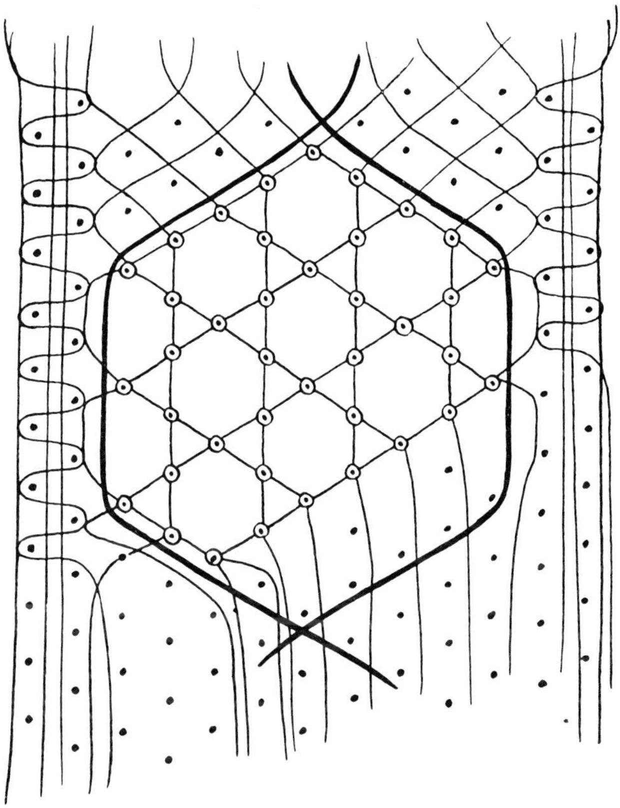

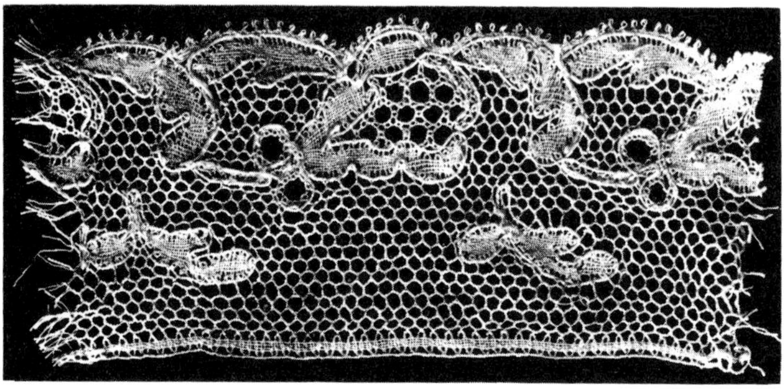

FLORAL PATTERNS

FLORAL patterns were popular in the first half of the nineteenth century. A few rules will be found applicable to any patterns of this type (For pricking see page 60).

Begin by working a little of the foot and ground, but do not let the work slope across the parchment at first, as the lace should have a straight and fairly even end. It will be found that at the top of the parchment each new row of ground is commenced with 2 couples (see diagram). Once the pattern is "set in" the method will be to keep as few bobbins as possible in use at one time, the bobbins not required for any section being pushed well to one side or to the back of the pillow. In very wide patterns bobbins not required for a time are tied tightly in bundles and turned back behind the work. To avoid time wasted in moving bobbins to begin a row of ground when needed for connection, work in V-shaped blocks as required, to bring it near a bud.

In working buds it will often be found necessary to add extra pairs to keep the cloth work close and firm. If left too thin, it is said by lacemakers to be "starved". When extra bobbins are required, tie 2 threads together, wind the knot a little way on to one of the bobbins, hang the connected pair over the working couple just before sticking a pin, then stick the pin and work back. When threads must be left out to make the ground, or to join one part of a bud to another, and the cloth work is so thin that they cannot be spared, the bobbins hung on to the worker close to the edge may be left out. If there are insufficient threads from the ground to begin a bud neatly, hang a couple on to the worker at the first pin stuck.

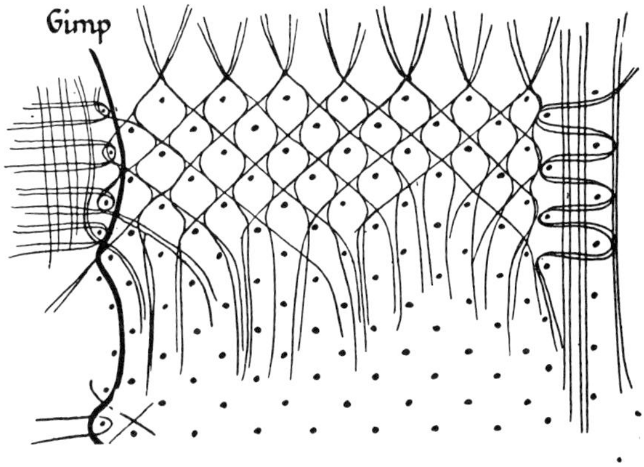

"Setting In" a wide Floral pattern.

When these extra pairs are no longer required, turn 1 couple at a time out of the cloth work back over the lace. These can be cut off and the loose ends trimmed when the pins are taken out.

To hang on gimps, connect the two bobbins and pass one bobbin of the joined pair, in and out through the couples which are ready to begin the bud. The first pin stuck will keep it in

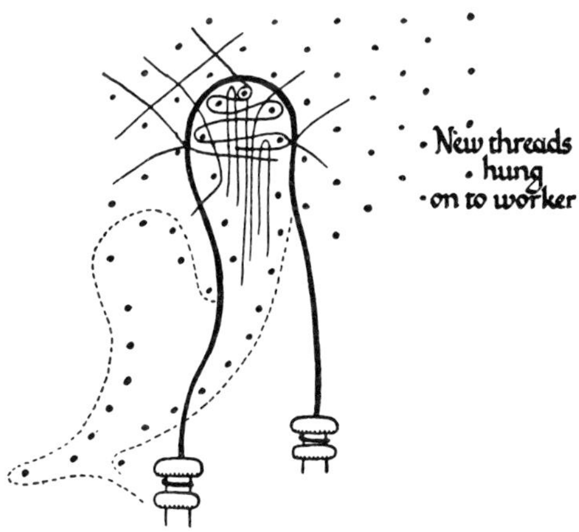

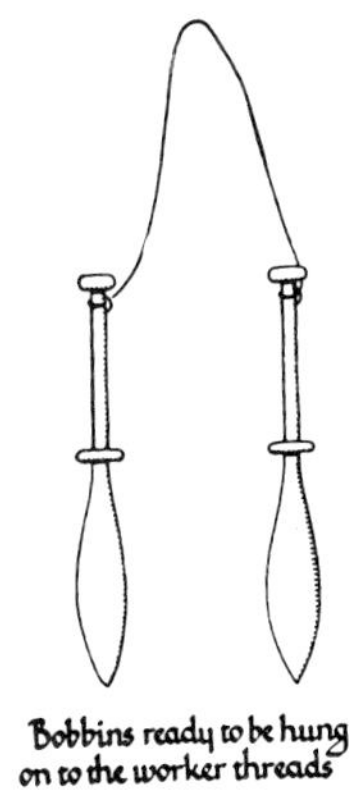

place. When gimps must be cut off at the end of a bud, one bobbin must be passed round through 2 or 3 couples, across the other gimp and doubling it; this will fix the gimps firmly, and they may be turned back out of the work and cut off when required elsewhere.

Sections of leaves below nookpins are finished separately, the most convenient pair being taken as a worker. Sections above the level of nookpins will be commenced separately. Chief difficulties likely to arise are (1) the tendency of the work to run askew. This must be corrected by sticking a pin twice in the same hole when necessary, since in cloth work the worker must travel straight across and the threads must lie parallel to each other. (2) The difficulty of seeing where to stick up when working a section of leaf or flower which must be finished before a gimp can be brought round it to a nookpin above. Then the nookpin hole can be used in the cloth work, and the pin taken out to stick up the gimp when the cloth work is finished.

The connecting of buds and ground will at first be very puzzling to the beginner accustomed only to geometrical forms. The eye must be trained to notice where a row of ground holes stops above or alongside the bud. If a row of ground continues *past* a bud, threads out of the bud must be left for it; these cannot be taken in again. If a row ends above the bud, the threads naturally come in to the bud from the ground. If the row ends at the side, a pair must be kept out to work the last hole of the row and taken in again at the next pin hole in the bud. If the holes come very close to the bud the worker from the bud can be used to finish the row and then take the worker straight back into the bud. If a part of a bud cannot be begun until another part is finished to bring the gimp round, bobbins must be hung on and left out from the part first worked in order to connect the 2 parts. To keep the ground even round a bud it may be advisable to continue a row of ground where no hole is pricked by working a ground stitch without sticking a pin.

On the head side, the principles explained in the honeycomb fan must be followed. Where the bud slopes away threads must be left out from the cloth work to be worked out afterwards for making headpins. Where cloth work is sloping outwards to the head side, the headpins must be made first and the couples worked in towards the cloth work. At the apex of the curves the worker from the cloth work will make the headpins.

A honeycomb ring may be begun at any convenient hole. From the first hole, one couple must go to the right and one to the left, care must be taken that they go in opposite directions to prevent a break in the ring. In working the other holes one couple must always be the one on the inside edge so that no threads are left lying across the ring. The other couple may be any of those coming into the ring, but it must be brought by means of whole stitches through any extra pairs that may lie inside the gimp. Threads brought in on the top side from the ground will be left out for the ground. The last hole is worked with the 2 inner pairs so that the ring is joined up. Threads not needed lie round the ring inside the gimp. A stem

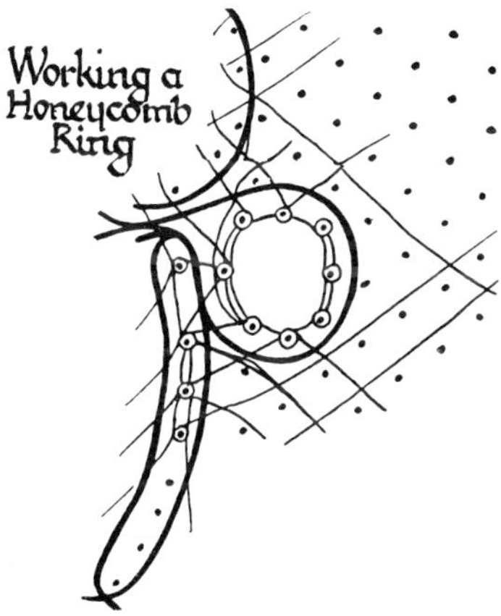

with honeycomb holes between 2 gimps is worked in the same way, extra pairs lie inside the gimps, and *one* pair must be carried on from hole to hole.

An experienced worker will exercise her own taste and judgment in working a pattern of this sort. There is much scope for ingenuity in arranging the gimps, in making the ground even round the buds, and in arranging the threads nicely round the rings.

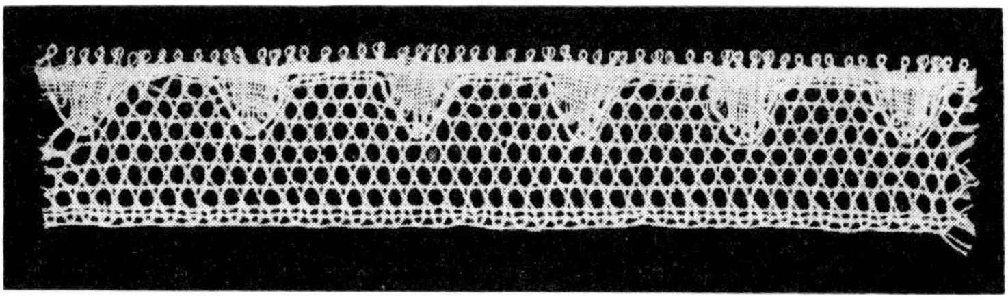

FRENCH GROUND EDGING

This pattern consists of French Ground or Kat stitch with a heading of cloth stitch border having V-shaped buds at intervals to encroach into the ground. The border is outlined by a gimp thread and the headpins are pearls or picots.

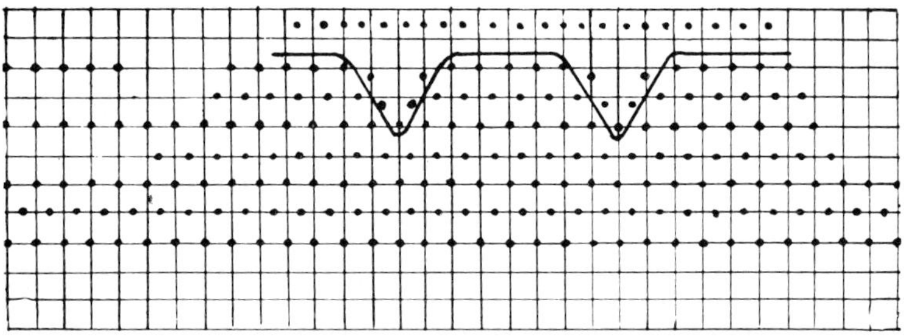

As has already been described, the diamond-shaped space between the 4 holes is longer in comparison with the point ground. Consequently 2 pairs of bobbins are required for each hole in working down a row.

Work the ground where the border is straight. Begin the foot as for point ground but twist the worker and each passive once. At the catchpin, work a whole stitch with the next pair, twist each pair once and stick a pin between the 2 pairs. Do not cover the pin. Use the left pair, carry on to the next pair, stick a pin as before, then work another pair without sticking a pin, and so on till the gimp line is reached. The last pair is used to work through the passive pairs of the border, headpin and back through the passives to the right. Work a whole stitch and twist with the first pair past the gimp. It will be seen that there are 2 pairs of bobbins hanging between each 2 pins. Work a whole stitch and twist with each of these 2 pairs. As there is no connection between these separate groups it is possible to work them from left to right, in the process of moving the bobbins to one side in order to begin the next line. The fourth pair from the right is the working pair to begin the foot in preparation for the next row. The foot may be worked with one twisted pair instead of two.

The ground will be worked round the bud in the heading and the couples go in and out of the bud as in point ground patterns, but owing to these couples lying in groups of two, it is a little more difficult to keep the ground round the bud a good shape. Be careful in working to leave out sufficient

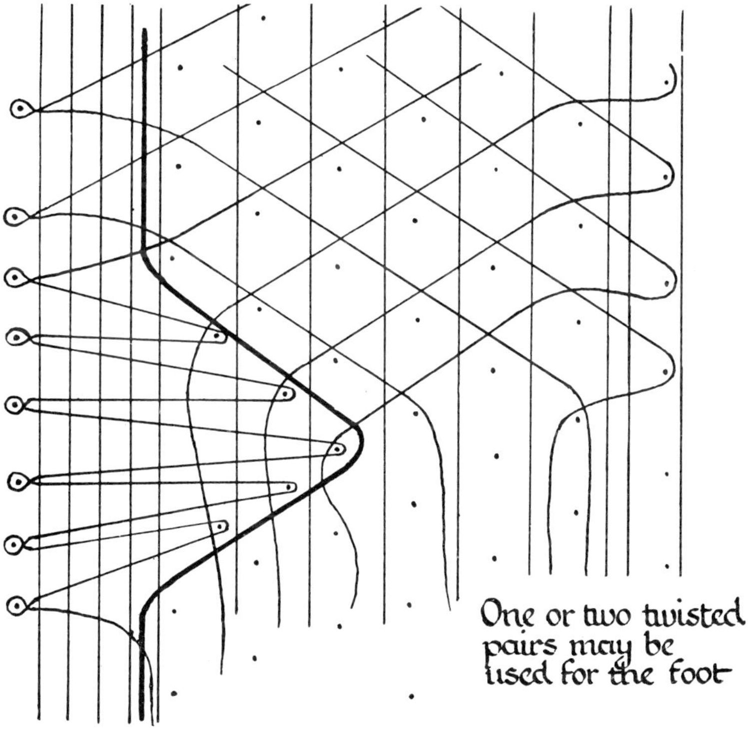

Each line represents a pair of bobbins.

bobbins to work the ground correctly before bringing the gimp round. If the rows of ground are worked alongside the bud it can easily be seen if the ground is working out correctly. Once the bud is finished no alteration can be made in the taking in and out of the pairs for the ground.

Note

The beginner must beware of forgetting the joining up of the 2 couples between 2 pins before beginning a row. In every case, in this ground, the bobbins are crossed after a stitch, and all stitches are whole stitches.

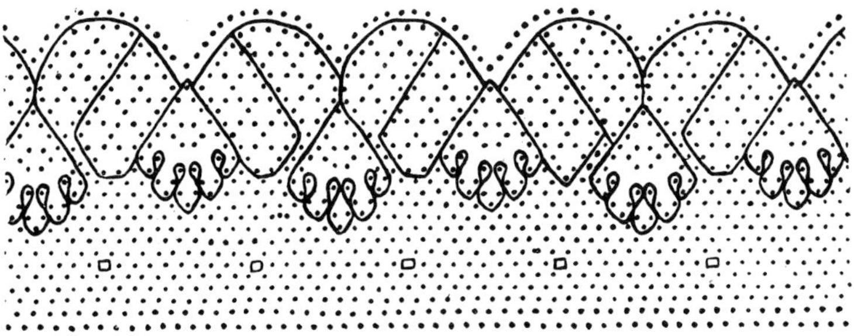

A fine old Buckinghamshire pattern.

Floral design.